W9-BMT-962

create™

Course Study Guide and Working Papers for College Accounting (Chapters 1-13), 15th Edition

John Price

create™

http://create.mheducation.com

Copyright 2018 by McGraw-Hill Education. All rights reserved. Printed in the United States of America. Except as permitted under the United States Copyright Act of 1976, no part of this publication may be reproduced or distributed in any form or by any means, or stored in a database or retrieval system, without prior written permission of the publisher.

This McGraw-Hill Create text may include materials submitted to McGraw-Hill for publication by the instructor of this course. The instructor is solely responsible for the editorial content of such materials. Instructors retain copyright of these additional materials.

ISBN-10: 125999502X ISBN-13: 9781259995026

Contents

Credits

WORKING PAPERS

Name ______________________________

CRITICAL THINKING PROBLEM

Copyright © 2017 by McGraw-Hill Education. All rights reserved.

WORKING PAPERS

Name ______________________________

EXERCISE 2.1

Assets ______________________________

Liabilities ______________________________

Owner's Equity ______________________________

EXERCISE 2.2

1. ______________________________
2. ______________________________
3. ______________________________
4. ______________________________
5. ______________________________

EXERCISE 2.3

	Assets	=	Liabilities	+	Owner's Equity
1.		=		+	
2.		=		+	
3.		=		+	
4.		=		+	
5.		=		+	
6.		=		+	
7.		=		+	
8.		=		+	
9.		=		+	
10.		=		+	

EXERCISE 2.4

Transaction	Assets	=	Liabilities	+	Owner's Equity
1.		=		+	
2.		=		+	
3.		=		+	
4.		=		+	
5.		=		+	

Copyright © 2017 by McGraw-Hill Education. All rights reserved.

Name ______________________

EXERCISE 2.5

	Assets			= Liabilities	+ Owner's Equity		
	Cash	+ Accounts Receivable	+ Equipment	= Accounts Payable	+ ______, Capital	+ Revenue	− Expenses
1.							
2.							
3.							
4.							
5.							
6.							
7.							
8.							
Totals		+	+	=	+	+	−

EXERCISE 2.6

____

Revenue

____

Expenses

____

EXERCISE 2.7

1. ______________________
2. ______________________
3. ______________________
4. ______________________
5. ______________________
6. ______________________
7. ______________________

Copyright © 2017 by McGraw-Hill Education. All rights reserved.

Name

EXERCISE 2.8

EXERCISE 2.9

Revenue

Expenses

Copyright © 2017 by McGraw-Hill Education. All rights reserved.

Name

EXERCISE 2.10

Copyright © 2017 by McGraw-Hill Education. All rights reserved.

Name

PROBLEM 2.1A or 2.1B

	Assets				=	Liabilities	+	Owner's Equity
	Cash	+ Accounts Receivable	+ Supplies	+ Equipment	=	Accounts Payable	+	Owner's Capital
1.								
2.								
3.								
4.								
5.								
6.								
7.								
8.								
9.								
10.								
11.								
Totals		+	+	+	=		+	

Analyze:

Copyright © 2017 by McGraw-Hill Education. All rights reserved.

Name ____________________

PROBLEM 2.2A or 2.2B

	Assets				= Liabilities +	Owner's Equity		
	Cash	+ Accounts Receivable	+	+	= Accounts Payable	+ Capital	+ Revenue	− Expenses
Beginning Balances		+	+	+	=	+	+	−
1.								
New Balances		+	+	+	=	+	+	−
2.								
New Balances		+	+	+	=	+	+	−
3.								
New Balances		+	+	+	=	+	+	−
4.								
New Balances		+	+	+	=	+	+	−
5.								
New Balances		+	+	+	=	+	+	−
6.								
New Balances		+	+	+	=	+	+	−
7.								
New Balances		+	+	+	=	+	+	−
8.								
New Balances		+	+	+	=	+	+	−
9.								
New Balances		+	+	+	=	+	+	−
10.								
New Balances		+	+	+	=	+	+	−

Analyze: ____________________

Copyright © 2017 by McGraw-Hill Education. All rights reserved.

Name

PROBLEM 2.3A or 2.3B

Analyze:

PROBLEM 2.4A or 2.4B

Copyright © 2017 by McGraw-Hill Education. All rights reserved.

Name

PROBLEM 2.4A or 2.4B (continued)

Analyze:

Copyright © 2017 by McGraw-Hill Education. All rights reserved.

Name

CRITICAL THINKING PROBLEM 2.1

Determine the balance for **William Giese**, April 30, 2019.

Assets			= Liabilities +	Owner's Equity			
Cash	+ Accounts Receivable	+ Machinery	= Accounts Payable	+ W. Giese Capital	− W. Giese Drawing	+ Revenue	− Expenses
$60,000	+ $24,000	+ $42,000	= $26,400	+ ?	− $13,600	+ $53,600	− $42,980

Let William Giese, Capital = X.

Solving for X:

William Giese, Capital, April 1, 2019 =	
Advertising Expense	$ 7,780
Maintenance Expense	9,200
Salaries Expense	26,000
Total Expenses	

Copyright © 2017 by McGraw-Hill Education. All rights reserved.

Name

CRITICAL THINKING PROBLEM 2.1 (continued)

Analyze:

Copyright © 2017 by McGraw-Hill Education. All rights reserved.

Name

CRITICAL THINKING PROBLEM 2.2

Copyright © 2017 by McGraw-Hill Education. All rights reserved.

WORKING PAPERS

Name ______________________

EXERCISE 3.1

EXERCISE 3.2

EXERCISE 3.3

1. ______________________
2. ______________________
3. ______________________
4. ______________________
5. ______________________
6. ______________________
7. ______________________
8. ______________________

Copyright © 2017 by McGraw-Hill Education. All rights reserved.

Name

EXERCISE 3.4

1.
2.
3.
4.
5.

EXERCISE 3.5

EXERCISE 3.6

ACCOUNT NAME	DEBIT	CREDIT

Copyright © 2017 by McGraw-Hill Education. All rights reserved.

Name

EXERCISE 3.6 (continued)

EXERCISE 3.7

Copyright © 2017 by McGraw-Hill Education. All rights reserved.

Name

EXERCISE 3.7 (continued)

EXERCISE 3.8

Copyright © 2017 by McGraw-Hill Education. All rights reserved.

Name ____________________

PROBLEM 3.1A or 3.1B

1.

2.

3.

4.

5.

6.

7.

8.

Analyze: ____________________

PROBLEM 3.2A or 3.2B

1.

2.

3.

4.

5.

6.

7.

8.

Analyze: ____________________

Copyright © 2017 by McGraw-Hill Education. All rights reserved.

Name

PROBLEM 3.3A or 3.3B

1.

2.

3.

4.

5.

6.

7.

8.

9.

10.

11.

12.

Copyright © 2017 by McGraw-Hill Education. All rights reserved.

Name ______________________

PROBLEM 3.4A or 3.4B

Analyze: ______________________

Copyright © 2017 by McGraw-Hill Education. All rights reserved.

Name

PROBLEM 3.5A or 3.5B

ACCOUNT NAME	DEBIT	CREDIT

Copyright © 2017 by McGraw-Hill Education. All rights reserved.

Name

PROBLEM 3.5A or 3.5B (continued)

Analyze:

Copyright © 2017 by McGraw-Hill Education. All rights reserved.

Name

CRITICAL THINKING PROBLEM 3.1

Copyright © 2017 by McGraw-Hill Education. All rights reserved.

Name ______________________

CRITICAL THINKING PROBLEM 3.1 (continued)

Copyright © 2017 by McGraw-Hill Education. All rights reserved.

Name

CRITICAL THINKING PROBLEM 3.1 (continued)

Copyright © 2017 by McGraw-Hill Education. All rights reserved.

Name

CRITICAL THINKING PROBLEM 3.2

Copyright © 2017 by McGraw-Hill Education. All rights reserved.

Name

CRITICAL THINKING PROBLEM 3.2 (continued)

ACCOUNT NAME	DEBIT	CREDIT

Copyright © 2017 by McGraw-Hill Education. All rights reserved.

Name

CRITICAL THINKING PROBLEM 3.2 (continued)

Analyze:

Copyright © 2017 by McGraw-Hill Education. All rights reserved.

WORKING PAPERS

Name ______________________________

EXERCISE 4.1

	Debit	Credit		Debit	Credit		Debit	Credit
1.			5.			8.		
2.			6.			9.		
3.			7.			10.		
4.								

EXERCISE 4.2

GENERAL JOURNAL

PAGE________

	DATE		DESCRIPTION	POST. REF.	DEBIT	CREDIT	
1							1
2							2
3							3
4							4
5							5
6							6
7							7
8							8
9							9
10							10
11							11
12							12
13							13
14							14
15							15
16							16
17							17
18							18
19							19
20							20
21							21
22							22
23							23
24							24
25							25
26							26
27							27
28							28
29							29

Copyright © 2017 by McGraw-Hill Education. All rights reserved.

Name ______________________________

EXERCISE 4.2 (continued)

GENERAL JOURNAL PAGE______

	DATE	DESCRIPTION	POST. REF.	DEBIT	CREDIT	
1						1
2						2
3						3
4						4
5						5
6						6
7						7
8						8
9						9
10						10
11						11
12						12
13						13
14						14
15						15
16						16

EXERCISE 4.3

GENERAL LEDGER

ACCOUNT ______________________________ ACCOUNT NO. __________

DATE	DESCRIPTION	POST. REF.	DEBIT	CREDIT	BALANCE	
					DEBIT	CREDIT

Copyright © 2017 by McGraw-Hill Education. All rights reserved.

Name ______________________

EXERCISE 4.3 (continued)

GENERAL LEDGER

ACCOUNT ______________________ ACCOUNT NO. ________

DATE		DESCRIPTION	POST. REF.	DEBIT	CREDIT	BALANCE DEBIT	BALANCE CREDIT

ACCOUNT ______________________ ACCOUNT NO. ________

DATE		DESCRIPTION	POST. REF.	DEBIT	CREDIT	BALANCE DEBIT	BALANCE CREDIT

ACCOUNT ______________________ ACCOUNT NO. ________

DATE		DESCRIPTION	POST. REF.	DEBIT	CREDIT	BALANCE DEBIT	BALANCE CREDIT

ACCOUNT ______________________ ACCOUNT NO. ________

DATE		DESCRIPTION	POST. REF.	DEBIT	CREDIT	BALANCE DEBIT	BALANCE CREDIT

ACCOUNT ______________________ ACCOUNT NO. ________

DATE		DESCRIPTION	POST. REF.	DEBIT	CREDIT	BALANCE DEBIT	BALANCE CREDIT

Copyright © 2017 by McGraw-Hill Education. All rights reserved.

Name ____________________

EXERCISE 4.3 (continued)

GENERAL LEDGER

ACCOUNT ____________________ ACCOUNT NO. ________

DATE		DESCRIPTION	POST. REF.	DEBIT	CREDIT	BALANCE	
						DEBIT	CREDIT

ACCOUNT ____________________ ACCOUNT NO. ________

DATE		DESCRIPTION	POST. REF.	DEBIT	CREDIT	BALANCE	
						DEBIT	CREDIT

ACCOUNT ____________________ ACCOUNT NO. ________

DATE		DESCRIPTION	POST. REF.	DEBIT	CREDIT	BALANCE	
						DEBIT	CREDIT

ACCOUNT ____________________ ACCOUNT NO. ________

DATE		DESCRIPTION	POST. REF.	DEBIT	CREDIT	BALANCE	
						DEBIT	CREDIT

ACCOUNT ____________________ ACCOUNT NO. ________

DATE		DESCRIPTION	POST. REF.	DEBIT	CREDIT	BALANCE	
						DEBIT	CREDIT

ACCOUNT ____________________ ACCOUNT NO. ________

DATE		DESCRIPTION	POST. REF.	DEBIT	CREDIT	BALANCE	
						DEBIT	CREDIT

Copyright © 2017 by McGraw-Hill Education. All rights reserved.

Name ______________________

EXERCISE 4.4

GENERAL JOURNAL PAGE ______

DATE	DESCRIPTION	POST. REF.	DEBIT	CREDIT

Copyright © 2017 by McGraw-Hill Education. All rights reserved.

Name

EXERCISE 4.5

GENERAL JOURNAL PAGE

	DATE		DESCRIPTION	POST. REF.	DEBIT	CREDIT	
1							1
2							2
3							3
4							4
5							5
6							6

EXERCISE 4.6

GENERAL JOURNAL PAGE

	DATE		DESCRIPTION	POST. REF.	DEBIT	CREDIT	
1							1
2							2
3							3
4							4
5							5
6							6

EXTRA FORM

GENERAL JOURNAL PAGE

	DATE		DESCRIPTION	POST. REF.	DEBIT	CREDIT	
1							1
2							2
3							3
4							4
5							5
6							6
7							7
8							8
9							9
10							10
11							11
12							12
13							13

Copyright © 2017 by McGraw-Hill Education. All rights reserved.

Name ____________________

PROBLEM 4.1A or 4.1B

GENERAL JOURNAL

PAGE ________

DATE	DESCRIPTION	POST. REF.	DEBIT	CREDIT

Copyright © 2017 by McGraw-Hill Education. All rights reserved.

Name ______________________

PROBLEM 4.1A or 4.1B (continued)

GENERAL JOURNAL

PAGE ______

DATE	DESCRIPTION	POST. REF.	DEBIT	CREDIT

Analyze: ______________________

Copyright © 2017 by McGraw-Hill Education. All rights reserved.

Name ____________________

PROBLEM 4.2A or 4.2B

GENERAL JOURNAL

PAGE ________

DATE	DESCRIPTION	POST. REF.	DEBIT	CREDIT

Copyright © 2017 by McGraw-Hill Education. All rights reserved.

Name ____________________

PROBLEM 4.2A or 4.2B (continued)

GENERAL JOURNAL PAGE ________

DATE		DESCRIPTION	POST. REF.	DEBIT	CREDIT

Copyright © 2017 by McGraw-Hill Education. All rights reserved.

Name

PROBLEM 4.2A or 4.2B (continued)

GENERAL LEDGER

ACCOUNT ______________________ ACCOUNT NO. ________

DATE		DESCRIPTION	POST. REF.	DEBIT	CREDIT	BALANCE DEBIT	BALANCE CREDIT

ACCOUNT ______________________ ACCOUNT NO. ________

DATE		DESCRIPTION	POST. REF.	DEBIT	CREDIT	BALANCE DEBIT	BALANCE CREDIT

ACCOUNT ______________________ ACCOUNT NO. ________

DATE		DESCRIPTION	POST. REF.	DEBIT	CREDIT	BALANCE DEBIT	BALANCE CREDIT

ACCOUNT ______________________ ACCOUNT NO. ________

DATE		DESCRIPTION	POST. REF.	DEBIT	CREDIT	BALANCE DEBIT	BALANCE CREDIT

Copyright © 2017 by McGraw-Hill Education. All rights reserved.

Name

PROBLEM 4.2A or 4.2B (continued)

GENERAL LEDGER

ACCOUNT ______ ACCOUNT NO. ______

DATE		DESCRIPTION	POST. REF.	DEBIT	CREDIT	BALANCE	
						DEBIT	CREDIT

ACCOUNT ______ ACCOUNT NO. ______

DATE		DESCRIPTION	POST. REF.	DEBIT	CREDIT	BALANCE	
						DEBIT	CREDIT

ACCOUNT ______ ACCOUNT NO. ______

DATE		DESCRIPTION	POST. REF.	DEBIT	CREDIT	BALANCE	
						DEBIT	CREDIT

ACCOUNT ______ ACCOUNT NO. ______

DATE		DESCRIPTION	POST. REF.	DEBIT	CREDIT	BALANCE	
						DEBIT	CREDIT

ACCOUNT ______ ACCOUNT NO. ______

DATE		DESCRIPTION	POST. REF.	DEBIT	CREDIT	BALANCE	
						DEBIT	CREDIT

Copyright © 2017 by McGraw-Hill Education. All rights reserved.

Name ______________________________

PROBLEM 4.2A or 4.2B (continued)

GENERAL LEDGER

ACCOUNT ______________________ ACCOUNT NO. __________

DATE	DESCRIPTION	POST. REF.	DEBIT	CREDIT	BALANCE	
					DEBIT	CREDIT

ACCOUNT ______________________ ACCOUNT NO. __________

DATE	DESCRIPTION	POST. REF.	DEBIT	CREDIT	BALANCE	
					DEBIT	CREDIT

ACCOUNT ______________________ ACCOUNT NO. __________

DATE	DESCRIPTION	POST. REF.	DEBIT	CREDIT	BALANCE	
					DEBIT	CREDIT

ACCOUNT ______________________ ACCOUNT NO. __________

DATE	DESCRIPTION	POST. REF.	DEBIT	CREDIT	BALANCE	
					DEBIT	CREDIT

ACCOUNT ______________________ ACCOUNT NO. __________

DATE	DESCRIPTION	POST. REF.	DEBIT	CREDIT	BALANCE	
					DEBIT	CREDIT

Analyze: ______________________________

Copyright © 2017 by McGraw-Hill Education. All rights reserved.

Name

PROBLEM 4.3A or 4.3B

Analyze:

PROBLEM 4.4A or 4.4B

GENERAL JOURNAL

PAGE

	DATE		DESCRIPTION	POST. REF.	DEBIT	CREDIT	
1							1
2							2
3							3
4							4
5							5
6							6
7							7
8							8
9							9
10							10
11							11
12							12
13							13
14							14
15							15
16							16
17							17
18							18
19							19
20							20
21							21
22							22
23							23
24							24
25							25
26							26

Copyright © 2017 by McGraw-Hill Education. All rights reserved.

Name

PROBLEM 4.4A or 4.4B (continued)

GENERAL LEDGER

ACCOUNT ______ ACCOUNT NO. ______

DATE		DESCRIPTION	POST. REF.	DEBIT	CREDIT	BALANCE DEBIT	BALANCE CREDIT

ACCOUNT ______ ACCOUNT NO. ______

DATE		DESCRIPTION	POST. REF.	DEBIT	CREDIT	BALANCE DEBIT	BALANCE CREDIT

ACCOUNT ______ ACCOUNT NO. ______

DATE		DESCRIPTION	POST. REF.	DEBIT	CREDIT	BALANCE DEBIT	BALANCE CREDIT

ACCOUNT ______ ACCOUNT NO. ______

DATE		DESCRIPTION	POST. REF.	DEBIT	CREDIT	BALANCE DEBIT	BALANCE CREDIT

ACCOUNT ______ ACCOUNT NO. ______

DATE		DESCRIPTION	POST. REF.	DEBIT	CREDIT	BALANCE DEBIT	BALANCE CREDIT

Copyright © 2017 by McGraw-Hill Education. All rights reserved.

Name

PROBLEM 4.4A or 4.4B (continued)

GENERAL LEDGER

ACCOUNT ______ ACCOUNT NO. ______

DATE		DESCRIPTION	POST. REF.	DEBIT	CREDIT	BALANCE DEBIT	BALANCE CREDIT

ACCOUNT ______ ACCOUNT NO. ______

DATE		DESCRIPTION	POST. REF.	DEBIT	CREDIT	BALANCE DEBIT	BALANCE CREDIT

ACCOUNT ______ ACCOUNT NO. ______

DATE		DESCRIPTION	POST. REF.	DEBIT	CREDIT	BALANCE DEBIT	BALANCE CREDIT

ACCOUNT ______ ACCOUNT NO. ______

DATE		DESCRIPTION	POST. REF.	DEBIT	CREDIT	BALANCE DEBIT	BALANCE CREDIT

Analyze: ______

EXTRA FORM

GENERAL LEDGER

ACCOUNT ______ ACCOUNT NO. ______

DATE		DESCRIPTION	POST. REF.	DEBIT	CREDIT	BALANCE DEBIT	BALANCE CREDIT

Copyright © 2017 by McGraw-Hill Education. All rights reserved.

Name

CRITICAL THINKING PROBLEM 4.1

Copyright © 2017 by McGraw-Hill Education. All rights reserved.

Name

CRITICAL THINKING PROBLEM 4.1 (continued)

Copyright © 2017 by McGraw-Hill Education. All rights reserved.

Name ____________________

CRITICAL THINKING PROBLEM 4.2

GENERAL JOURNAL

PAGE ________

DATE	DESCRIPTION	POST. REF.	DEBIT	CREDIT

Copyright © 2017 by McGraw-Hill Education. All rights reserved.

Name ______________________________

CRITICAL THINKING PROBLEM 4.2 (continued)

GENERAL JOURNAL PAGE________

DATE	DESCRIPTION	POST. REF.	DEBIT	CREDIT

Copyright © 2017 by McGraw-Hill Education. All rights reserved.

Name ____________________

CRITICAL THINKING PROBLEM 4.2 (continued)

GENERAL JOURNAL

PAGE ________

	DATE	DESCRIPTION	POST. REF.	DEBIT	CREDIT	
1						1
2						2
3						3
4						4
5						5
6						6
7						7
8						8
9						9
10						10
11						11
12						12
13						13
14						14

GENERAL LEDGER

ACCOUNT ______________________________ ACCOUNT NO. __________

DATE	DESCRIPTION	POST. REF.	DEBIT	CREDIT	BALANCE	
					DEBIT	CREDIT

Copyright © 2017 by McGraw-Hill Education. All rights reserved.

Name ______________________________

CRITICAL THINKING PROBLEM 4.2 (continued)

GENERAL LEDGER

ACCOUNT ______________________________ ACCOUNT NO. __________

DATE	DESCRIPTION	POST. REF.	DEBIT	CREDIT	BALANCE DEBIT	BALANCE CREDIT

ACCOUNT ______________________________ ACCOUNT NO. __________

DATE	DESCRIPTION	POST. REF.	DEBIT	CREDIT	BALANCE DEBIT	BALANCE CREDIT

ACCOUNT ______________________________ ACCOUNT NO. __________

DATE	DESCRIPTION	POST. REF.	DEBIT	CREDIT	BALANCE DEBIT	BALANCE CREDIT

ACCOUNT ______________________________ ACCOUNT NO. __________

DATE	DESCRIPTION	POST. REF.	DEBIT	CREDIT	BALANCE DEBIT	BALANCE CREDIT

ACCOUNT ______________________________ ACCOUNT NO. __________

DATE	DESCRIPTION	POST. REF.	DEBIT	CREDIT	BALANCE DEBIT	BALANCE CREDIT

Copyright © 2017 by McGraw-Hill Education. All rights reserved.

Name ______________________________

CRITICAL THINKING PROBLEM 4.2 (continued)

GENERAL LEDGER

ACCOUNT ______________________________ ACCOUNT NO. __________

DATE		DESCRIPTION	POST. REF.	DEBIT	CREDIT	BALANCE	
						DEBIT	CREDIT

ACCOUNT ______________________________ ACCOUNT NO. __________

DATE		DESCRIPTION	POST. REF.	DEBIT	CREDIT	BALANCE	
						DEBIT	CREDIT

ACCOUNT ______________________________ ACCOUNT NO. __________

DATE		DESCRIPTION	POST. REF.	DEBIT	CREDIT	BALANCE	
						DEBIT	CREDIT

ACCOUNT ______________________________ ACCOUNT NO. __________

DATE		DESCRIPTION	POST. REF.	DEBIT	CREDIT	BALANCE	
						DEBIT	CREDIT

ACCOUNT ______________________________ ACCOUNT NO. __________

DATE		DESCRIPTION	POST. REF.	DEBIT	CREDIT	BALANCE	
						DEBIT	CREDIT

Copyright © 2017 by McGraw-Hill Education. All rights reserved.

Name ____________________

CRITICAL THINKING PROBLEM 4.2 (continued)

GENERAL LEDGER

ACCOUNT ____________________ ACCOUNT NO. ________

DATE	DESCRIPTION	POST. REF.	DEBIT	CREDIT	BALANCE DEBIT	BALANCE CREDIT

ACCOUNT ____________________ ACCOUNT NO. ________

DATE	DESCRIPTION	POST. REF.	DEBIT	CREDIT	BALANCE DEBIT	BALANCE CREDIT

ACCOUNT ____________________ ACCOUNT NO. ________

DATE	DESCRIPTION	POST. REF.	DEBIT	CREDIT	BALANCE DEBIT	BALANCE CREDIT

EXTRA FORMS

GENERAL LEDGER

ACCOUNT ____________________ ACCOUNT NO. ________

DATE	DESCRIPTION	POST. REF.	DEBIT	CREDIT	BALANCE DEBIT	BALANCE CREDIT

ACCOUNT ____________________ ACCOUNT NO. ________

DATE	DESCRIPTION	POST. REF.	DEBIT	CREDIT	BALANCE DEBIT	BALANCE CREDIT

Copyright © 2017 by McGraw-Hill Education. All rights reserved.

Name

CRITICAL THINKING PROBLEM 4.2 (continued)

ACCOUNT NAME	DEBIT	CREDIT

Copyright © 2017 by McGraw-Hill Education. All rights reserved.

Name ______________________

CRITICAL THINKING PROBLEM 4.2 (continued)

Analyze: ______________________

Copyright © 2017 by McGraw-Hill Education. All rights reserved.

WORKING PAPERS

Name ______________________

EXERCISE 5.1

1. ______________________

2. ______________________

3. ______________________

EXERCISE 5.2

1. ______________________

2. ______________________

Copyright © 2017 by McGraw-Hill Education. All rights reserved.

Name ____________________

EXERCISE 5.3

	ACCOUNT NAME	TRIAL BALANCE		ADJUSTMENTS		ADJUSTED TRIAL BALANCE		
		DEBIT	CREDIT	DEBIT	CREDIT	DEBIT	CREDIT	
1								1
2								2
3								3
4								4
5								5
6								6
7								7
8								8
9								9
10								10
11								11
12								12
13								13
14								14
15								15
16								16
17								17
18								18
19								19
20								20
21								21
22								22

Copyright © 2017 by McGraw-Hill Education. All rights reserved.

Name

EXERCISE 5.4

Copyright © 2017 by McGraw-Hill Education. All rights reserved.

Name ____________________

EXERCISE 5.5

GENERAL JOURNAL

PAGE ________

	DATE		DESCRIPTION	POST. REF.	DEBIT	CREDIT	
1							1
2							2
3							3
4							4
5							5
6							6
7							7
8							8
9							9
10							10
11							11

GENERAL LEDGER

ACCOUNT **Supplies** ACCOUNT NO. **121**

DATE		DESCRIPTION	POST. REF.	DEBIT	CREDIT	BALANCE DEBIT	BALANCE CREDIT

ACCOUNT **Prepaid Insurance** ACCOUNT NO. **131**

DATE		DESCRIPTION	POST. REF.	DEBIT	CREDIT	BALANCE DEBIT	BALANCE CREDIT

ACCOUNT **Accumulated Depreciation—Equipment** ACCOUNT NO. **142**

DATE		DESCRIPTION	POST. REF.	DEBIT	CREDIT	BALANCE DEBIT	BALANCE CREDIT

Copyright © 2017 by McGraw-Hill Education. All rights reserved.

Name ______________________

EXERCISE 5.5 (continued)

GENERAL LEDGER

ACCOUNT **Depreciation Expense—Equipment** ACCOUNT NO. **517**

DATE	DESCRIPTION	POST. REF.	DEBIT	CREDIT	BALANCE DEBIT	BALANCE CREDIT

ACCOUNT **Insurance Expense** ACCOUNT NO. **521**

DATE	DESCRIPTION	POST. REF.	DEBIT	CREDIT	BALANCE DEBIT	BALANCE CREDIT

ACCOUNT **Supplies Expense** ACCOUNT NO. **523**

DATE	DESCRIPTION	POST. REF.	DEBIT	CREDIT	BALANCE DEBIT	BALANCE CREDIT

EXTRA FORMS

ACCOUNT ______________________ ACCOUNT NO. ________

DATE	DESCRIPTION	POST. REF.	DEBIT	CREDIT	BALANCE DEBIT	BALANCE CREDIT

ACCOUNT ______________________ ACCOUNT NO. ________

DATE	DESCRIPTION	POST. REF.	DEBIT	CREDIT	BALANCE DEBIT	BALANCE CREDIT

Copyright © 2017 by McGraw-Hill Education. All rights reserved.

Name

PROBLEM 5.1A or 5.1B

	ACCOUNT NAME	TRIAL BALANCE		ADJUSTMENTS	
		DEBIT	CREDIT	DEBIT	CREDIT
1					
2					
3					
4					
5					
6					
7					
8					
9					
10					
11					
12					
13					
14					
15					
16					
17					
18					
19					
20					
21					
22					
23					
24					
25					
26					
27					
28					
29					
30					
31					
32					

Copyright © 2017 by McGraw-Hill Education. All rights reserved.

Name ______________________

PROBLEM 5.1A or 5.1B (continued)

ADJUSTED TRIAL BALANCE		INCOME STATEMENT		BALANCE SHEET	
DEBIT	CREDIT	DEBIT	CREDIT	DEBIT	CREDIT

Analyze: ______________________

Copyright © 2017 by McGraw-Hill Education. All rights reserved.

Name

PROBLEM 5.2A or 5.2B

	ACCOUNT NAME	TRIAL BALANCE		ADJUSTMENTS	
		DEBIT	CREDIT	DEBIT	CREDIT
1					
2					
3					
4					
5					
6					
7					
8					
9					
10					
11					
12					
13					
14					
15					
16					
17					
18					
19					
20					
21					
22					
23					
24					
25					
26					
27					
28					
29					
30					
31					
32					

Copyright © 2017 by McGraw-Hill Education. All rights reserved.

Name

PROBLEM 5.2A or 5.2B (continued)

ADJUSTED TRIAL BALANCE		INCOME STATEMENT		BALANCE SHEET		
DEBIT	CREDIT	DEBIT	CREDIT	DEBIT	CREDIT	
						1
						2
						3
						4
						5
						6
						7
						8
						9
						10
						11
						12
						13
						14
						15
						16
						17
						18
						19
						20
						21
						22
						23
						24
						25
						26
						27
						28
						29
						30
						31
						32

Analyze:

Copyright © 2017 by McGraw-Hill Education. All rights reserved.

Name

PROBLEM 5.3A or 5.3B

Copyright © 2017 by McGraw-Hill Education. All rights reserved.

Name

PROBLEM 5.3A or 5.3B (continued)

Analyze:

Copyright © 2017 by McGraw-Hill Education. All rights reserved.

Name ____________________

PROBLEM 5.4A or 5.4B

	ACCOUNT NAME	TRIAL BALANCE DEBIT	TRIAL BALANCE CREDIT	ADJUSTMENTS DEBIT	ADJUSTMENTS CREDIT
1					
2					
3					
4					
5					
6					
7					
8					
9					
10					
11					
12					
13					
14					
15					
16					
17					
18					
19					
20					
21					
22					
23					
24					
25					
26					
27					
28					
29					
30					
31					
32					

Copyright © 2017 by McGraw-Hill Education. All rights reserved.

Name

PROBLEM 5.4A or 5.4B (continued)

ADJUSTED TRIAL BALANCE		INCOME STATEMENT		BALANCE SHEET		
DEBIT	CREDIT	DEBIT	CREDIT	DEBIT	CREDIT	
						1
						2
						3
						4
						5
						6
						7
						8
						9
						10
						11
						12
						13
						14
						15
						16
						17
						18
						19
						20
						21
						22
						23
						24
						25
						26
						27
						28
						29
						30
						31
						32

Copyright © 2017 by McGraw-Hill Education. All rights reserved.

Name

PROBLEM 5.4A or 5.4B (continued)

Copyright © 2017 by McGraw-Hill Education. All rights reserved.

Name

PROBLEM 5.4A or 5.4B (continued)

Copyright © 2017 by McGraw-Hill Education. All rights reserved.

Name ____________________

PROBLEM 5.4A or 5.4B (continued)

GENERAL JOURNAL

PAGE______

	DATE		DESCRIPTION	POST. REF.	DEBIT	CREDIT	
1							1
2							2
3							3
4							4
5							5
6							6
7							7
8							8
9							9
10							10
11							11
12							12
13							13
14							14

GENERAL LEDGER

ACCOUNT ____________________ ACCOUNT NO. ________

DATE		DESCRIPTION	POST. REF.	DEBIT	CREDIT	BALANCE	
						DEBIT	CREDIT

ACCOUNT ____________________ ACCOUNT NO. ________

DATE		DESCRIPTION	POST. REF.	DEBIT	CREDIT	BALANCE	
						DEBIT	CREDIT

ACCOUNT ____________________ ACCOUNT NO. ________

DATE		DESCRIPTION	POST. REF.	DEBIT	CREDIT	BALANCE	
						DEBIT	CREDIT

Copyright © 2017 by McGraw-Hill Education. All rights reserved.

Name ____________________

PROBLEM 5.4A or 5.4B (continued)

GENERAL LEDGER

ACCOUNT ____________________ ACCOUNT NO. ________

DATE		DESCRIPTION	POST. REF.	DEBIT	CREDIT	BALANCE	
						DEBIT	CREDIT

ACCOUNT ____________________ ACCOUNT NO. ________

DATE		DESCRIPTION	POST. REF.	DEBIT	CREDIT	BALANCE	
						DEBIT	CREDIT

ACCOUNT ____________________ ACCOUNT NO. ________

DATE		DESCRIPTION	POST. REF.	DEBIT	CREDIT	BALANCE	
						DEBIT	CREDIT

ACCOUNT ____________________ ACCOUNT NO. ________

DATE		DESCRIPTION	POST. REF.	DEBIT	CREDIT	BALANCE	
						DEBIT	CREDIT

ACCOUNT ____________________ ACCOUNT NO. ________

DATE		DESCRIPTION	POST. REF.	DEBIT	CREDIT	BALANCE	
						DEBIT	CREDIT

Analyze: ____________________

____

Copyright © 2017 by McGraw-Hill Education. All rights reserved.

Name

CRITICAL THINKING PROBLEM 5.1

TO:

FROM:

DATE:

SUBJECT:

Copyright © 2017 by McGraw-Hill Education. All rights reserved.

Name

CRITICAL THINKING PROBLEM 5.2

	ACCOUNT NAME	TRIAL BALANCE DEBIT	TRIAL BALANCE CREDIT	ADJUSTMENTS DEBIT	ADJUSTMENTS CREDIT
1					
2					
3					
4					
5					
6					
7					
8					
9					
10					
11					
12					
13					
14					
15					
16					
17					
18					
19					
20					
21					
22					
23					
24					
25					
26					
27					
28					
29					
30					
31					
32					

Copyright © 2017 by McGraw-Hill Education. All rights reserved.

Name ______________________________

CRITICAL THINKING PROBLEM 5.2 (continued)

	ADJUSTED TRIAL BALANCE		INCOME STATEMENT		BALANCE SHEET		
	DEBIT	CREDIT	DEBIT	CREDIT	DEBIT	CREDIT	
							1
							2
							3
							4
							5
							6
							7
							8
							9
							10
							11
							12
							13
							14
							15
							16
							17
							18
							19
							20
							21
							22
							23
							24
							25
							26
							27
							28
							29
							30
							31
							32

Copyright © 2017 by McGraw-Hill Education. All rights reserved.

Name

CRITICAL THINKING PROBLEM 5.2 (continued)

Copyright © 2017 by McGraw-Hill Education. All rights reserved.

Name

CRITICAL THINKING PROBLEM 5.2 (continued)

Copyright © 2017 by McGraw-Hill Education. All rights reserved.

Name

CRITICAL THINKING PROBLEM 5.2 (continued)

GENERAL JOURNAL

PAGE

	DATE		DESCRIPTION	POST. REF.	DEBIT	CREDIT	
1							1
2							2
3							3
4							4
5							5
6							6
7							7
8							8
9							9
10							10
11							11

GENERAL LEDGER

ACCOUNT ACCOUNT NO.

DATE		DESCRIPTION	POST. REF.	DEBIT	CREDIT	BALANCE	
						DEBIT	CREDIT

ACCOUNT ACCOUNT NO.

DATE		DESCRIPTION	POST. REF.	DEBIT	CREDIT	BALANCE	
						DEBIT	CREDIT

ACCOUNT ACCOUNT NO.

DATE		DESCRIPTION	POST. REF.	DEBIT	CREDIT	BALANCE	
						DEBIT	CREDIT

Copyright © 2017 by McGraw-Hill Education. All rights reserved.

Name

CRITICAL THINKING PROBLEM 5.2 (continued)

GENERAL LEDGER

ACCOUNT ______ ACCOUNT NO. ______

DATE		DESCRIPTION	POST. REF.	DEBIT	CREDIT	BALANCE DEBIT	BALANCE CREDIT

ACCOUNT ______ ACCOUNT NO. ______

DATE		DESCRIPTION	POST. REF.	DEBIT	CREDIT	BALANCE DEBIT	BALANCE CREDIT

ACCOUNT ______ ACCOUNT NO. ______

DATE		DESCRIPTION	POST. REF.	DEBIT	CREDIT	BALANCE DEBIT	BALANCE CREDIT

Analyze: ______

EXTRA FORMS

ACCOUNT ______ ACCOUNT NO. ______

DATE		DESCRIPTION	POST. REF.	DEBIT	CREDIT	BALANCE DEBIT	BALANCE CREDIT

ACCOUNT ______ ACCOUNT NO. ______

DATE		DESCRIPTION	POST. REF.	DEBIT	CREDIT	BALANCE DEBIT	BALANCE CREDIT

Copyright © 2017 by McGraw-Hill Education. All rights reserved.

WORKING PAPERS

Name ______________________________

EXERCISE 6.1

GENERAL JOURNAL PAGE ________

	DATE	DESCRIPTION	POST. REF.	DEBIT	CREDIT	
1						1
2						2
3						3
4						4
5						5
6						6
7						7
8						8
9						9
10						10
11						11
12						12
13						13
14						14
15						15
16						16
17						17
18						18
19						19
20						20
21						21

EXERCISE 6.2

1. ______________________________
2. ______________________________
3. ______________________________
4. ______________________________
5. ______________________________
6. ______________________________
7. ______________________________
8. ______________________________
9. ______________________________

Copyright © 2017 by McGraw-Hill Education. All rights reserved.

Name ______________________________

EXERCISE 6.3

1. ______________________
2. ______________________
3. ______________________
4. ______________________
5. ______________________
6. ______________________
7. ______________________

EXERCISE 6.4

1. ______________
2. ______________
3. ______________
4. ______________
5. ______________
6. ______________
7. ______________
8. ______________
9. ______________
10. ______________
11. ______________
12. ______________
13. ______________
14. ______________
15. ______________

EXERCISE 6.5

1. Total revenue for the period is __________.

2. Total expenses for the period are __________.

3. Net income for the period is __________.

4. Owner's withdrawals for the period are __________.

Copyright © 2017 by McGraw-Hill Education. All rights reserved.

Name

EXERCISE 6.6

GENERAL JOURNAL PAGE

DATE		DESCRIPTION	POST. REF.	DEBIT	CREDIT

Copyright © 2017 by McGraw-Hill Education. All rights reserved.

Name ____________________

GENERAL LEDGER

ACCOUNT **Aretha Hinkle, Capital** ACCOUNT NO. **301**

DATE		DESCRIPTION	POST. REF.	DEBIT	CREDIT	BALANCE DEBIT	BALANCE CREDIT
2019							
Mar.	**31**	**Balance**	✓				**65 0 0 0 00**

ACCOUNT **Aretha Hinkle, Drawing** ACCOUNT NO. **302**

DATE		DESCRIPTION	POST. REF.	DEBIT	CREDIT	BALANCE DEBIT	BALANCE CREDIT
2019							
Mar.	**31**	**Balance**	✓			**6 5 0 0 00**	

ACCOUNT **Income Summary** ACCOUNT NO. **399**

DATE		DESCRIPTION	POST. REF.	DEBIT	CREDIT	BALANCE DEBIT	BALANCE CREDIT

ACCOUNT **Fees Income** ACCOUNT NO. **401**

DATE		DESCRIPTION	POST. REF.	DEBIT	CREDIT	BALANCE DEBIT	BALANCE CREDIT
2019							
Mar.	**31**	**Balance**	✓				**187 2 3 0 00**

ACCOUNT **Depreciation Expense—Equipment** ACCOUNT NO. **510**

DATE		DESCRIPTION	POST. REF.	DEBIT	CREDIT	BALANCE DEBIT	BALANCE CREDIT
2019							
Mar.	**31**	**Balance**	✓			**10 5 8 0 00**	

Copyright © 2017 by McGraw-Hill Education. All rights reserved.

Name ______________________________

EXERCISE 6.6 (continued)

GENERAL LEDGER

ACCOUNT Insurance Expense ACCOUNT NO. 511

DATE		DESCRIPTION	POST. REF.	DEBIT	CREDIT	BALANCE DEBIT	BALANCE CREDIT
2019							
Mar.	31	Balance	✓			5,700.00	

ACCOUNT Rent Expense ACCOUNT NO. 514

DATE		DESCRIPTION	POST. REF.	DEBIT	CREDIT	BALANCE DEBIT	BALANCE CREDIT
2019							
Mar.	31	Balance	✓			16,500.00	

ACCOUNT Salaries Expense ACCOUNT NO. 517

DATE		DESCRIPTION	POST. REF.	DEBIT	CREDIT	BALANCE DEBIT	BALANCE CREDIT
2019							
Mar.	31	Balance	✓			83,000.00	

ACCOUNT Supplies Expense ACCOUNT NO. 518

DATE		DESCRIPTION	POST. REF.	DEBIT	CREDIT	BALANCE DEBIT	BALANCE CREDIT
2019							
Mar.	31	Balance	✓			2,800.00	

ACCOUNT Telephone Expense ACCOUNT NO. 519

DATE		DESCRIPTION	POST. REF.	DEBIT	CREDIT	BALANCE DEBIT	BALANCE CREDIT
2019							
Mar.	31	Balance	✓			3,400.00	

Copyright © 2017 by McGraw-Hill Education. All rights reserved.

Name ______________________________

EXERCISE 6.6 (continued)

GENERAL LEDGER

ACCOUNT **Utilities Expense** ACCOUNT NO. **523**

DATE		DESCRIPTION	POST. REF.	DEBIT	CREDIT	BALANCE DEBIT	BALANCE CREDIT
2019							
Mar.	**31**	**Balance**	✓			**4 7 0 0 00**	

EXTRA FORMS

ACCOUNT ______________________ ACCOUNT NO. __________

DATE		DESCRIPTION	POST. REF.	DEBIT	CREDIT	BALANCE DEBIT	BALANCE CREDIT

ACCOUNT ______________________ ACCOUNT NO. __________

DATE		DESCRIPTION	POST. REF.	DEBIT	CREDIT	BALANCE DEBIT	BALANCE CREDIT

ACCOUNT ______________________ ACCOUNT NO. __________

DATE		DESCRIPTION	POST. REF.	DEBIT	CREDIT	BALANCE DEBIT	BALANCE CREDIT

Copyright © 2017 by McGraw-Hill Education. All rights reserved.

Name ____________________

EXERCISE 6.7

GENERAL JOURNAL PAGE________

	DATE	DESCRIPTION	POST. REF.	DEBIT	CREDIT	
1						1
2						2
3						3
4						4
5						5
6						6
7						7
8						8

EXERCISE 6.8

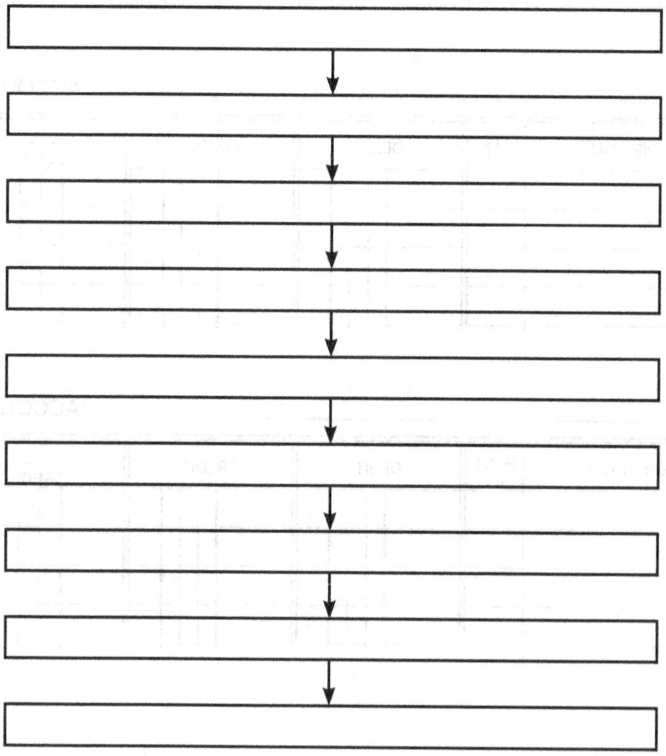

Copyright © 2017 by McGraw-Hill Education. All rights reserved.

Name

PROBLEM 6.1A or 6.1B

GENERAL JOURNAL

PAGE

DATE		DESCRIPTION	POST. REF.	DEBIT	CREDIT

GENERAL JOURNAL

PAGE

DATE		DESCRIPTION	POST. REF.	DEBIT	CREDIT

Analyze:

Copyright © 2017 by McGraw-Hill Education. All rights reserved.

Name ______________________________

PROBLEM 6.2A or 6.2B

GENERAL JOURNAL — PAGE ________

	DATE		DESCRIPTION	POST. REF.	DEBIT	CREDIT	
1							1
2							2
3							3
4							4
5							5
6							6
7							7
8							8
9							9
10							10
11							11

GENERAL JOURNAL — PAGE ________

	DATE		DESCRIPTION	POST. REF.	DEBIT	CREDIT	
1							1
2							2
3							3
4							4
5							5
6							6
7							7
8							8
9							9
10							10
11							11
12							12
13							13
14							14
15							15
16							16
17							17
18							18

Copyright © 2017 by McGraw-Hill Education. All rights reserved.

Name

PROBLEM 6.2A or 6.2B (continued)

GENERAL LEDGER

ACCOUNT **Supplies** ACCOUNT NO. **121**

DATE		DESCRIPTION	POST. REF.	DEBIT	CREDIT	BALANCE DEBIT	BALANCE CREDIT

ACCOUNT **Prepaid Advertising** ACCOUNT NO. **131**

DATE		DESCRIPTION	POST. REF.	DEBIT	CREDIT	BALANCE DEBIT	BALANCE CREDIT

ACCOUNT **Accumulated Depreciation—Equipment** ACCOUNT NO. **142**

DATE		DESCRIPTION	POST. REF.	DEBIT	CREDIT	BALANCE DEBIT	BALANCE CREDIT

ACCOUNT **Capital** ACCOUNT NO. **301**

DATE		DESCRIPTION	POST. REF.	DEBIT	CREDIT	BALANCE DEBIT	BALANCE CREDIT

ACCOUNT **Drawing** ACCOUNT NO. **302**

DATE		DESCRIPTION	POST. REF.	DEBIT	CREDIT	BALANCE DEBIT	BALANCE CREDIT

Copyright © 2017 by McGraw-Hill Education. All rights reserved.

Name

PROBLEM 6.2A or 6.2B (continued)

GENERAL LEDGER

ACCOUNT **Income Summary** ACCOUNT NO. **399**

DATE	DESCRIPTION	POST. REF.	DEBIT	CREDIT	BALANCE DEBIT	BALANCE CREDIT

ACCOUNT **Fees Income** ACCOUNT NO. **401**

DATE	DESCRIPTION	POST. REF.	DEBIT	CREDIT	BALANCE DEBIT	BALANCE CREDIT

GENERAL LEDGER

ACCOUNT **Salaries Expense** ACCOUNT NO. **511**

DATE	DESCRIPTION	POST. REF.	DEBIT	CREDIT	BALANCE DEBIT	BALANCE CREDIT

ACCOUNT **Utilities Expense** ACCOUNT NO. **514**

DATE	DESCRIPTION	POST. REF.	DEBIT	CREDIT	BALANCE DEBIT	BALANCE CREDIT

ACCOUNT **Supplies Expense** ACCOUNT NO. **517**

DATE	DESCRIPTION	POST. REF.	DEBIT	CREDIT	BALANCE DEBIT	BALANCE CREDIT

Copyright © 2017 by McGraw-Hill Education. All rights reserved.

Name

PROBLEM 6.2A or 6.2B (continued)

ACCOUNT Depreciation Expense—Equipment ACCOUNT NO. 523

DATE		DESCRIPTION	POST. REF.	DEBIT	CREDIT	BALANCE DEBIT	BALANCE CREDIT

ACCOUNT Advertising Expense ACCOUNT NO. 526

DATE		DESCRIPTION	POST. REF.	DEBIT	CREDIT	BALANCE DEBIT	BALANCE CREDIT

ACCOUNT NAME	DEBIT	CREDIT

Analyze:

Copyright © 2017 by McGraw-Hill Education. All rights reserved.

Name ______________________

PROBLEM 6.3A or 6.3B

GENERAL JOURNAL PAGE______

DATE		DESCRIPTION	POST. REF.	DEBIT	CREDIT

Copyright © 2017 by McGraw-Hill Education. All rights reserved.

Name

PROBLEM 6.3A or 6.3B (continued)

GENERAL LEDGER

ACCOUNT Capital ACCOUNT NO. 301

DATE		DESCRIPTION	POST. REF.	DEBIT	CREDIT	BALANCE DEBIT	BALANCE CREDIT

ACCOUNT Drawing ACCOUNT NO. 302

DATE		DESCRIPTION	POST. REF.	DEBIT	CREDIT	BALANCE DEBIT	BALANCE CREDIT

ACCOUNT Income Summary ACCOUNT NO. 399

DATE		DESCRIPTION	POST. REF.	DEBIT	CREDIT	BALANCE DEBIT	BALANCE CREDIT

ACCOUNT Fees Income ACCOUNT NO. 401

DATE		DESCRIPTION	POST. REF.	DEBIT	CREDIT	BALANCE DEBIT	BALANCE CREDIT

Copyright © 2017 by McGraw-Hill Education. All rights reserved.

Name

PROBLEM 6.3A or 6.3B (continued)

GENERAL LEDGER

ACCOUNT **Advertising Expense** ACCOUNT NO. **511**

DATE	DESCRIPTION	POST. REF.	DEBIT	CREDIT	BALANCE DEBIT	BALANCE CREDIT

ACCOUNT **Depreciation Expense—Equipment** ACCOUNT NO. **514**

DATE	DESCRIPTION	POST. REF.	DEBIT	CREDIT	BALANCE DEBIT	BALANCE CREDIT

ACCOUNT **Rent Expense** ACCOUNT NO. **517**

DATE	DESCRIPTION	POST. REF.	DEBIT	CREDIT	BALANCE DEBIT	BALANCE CREDIT

ACCOUNT **Salaries Expense** ACCOUNT NO. **519**

DATE	DESCRIPTION	POST. REF.	DEBIT	CREDIT	BALANCE DEBIT	BALANCE CREDIT

ACCOUNT **Utilities Expense** ACCOUNT NO. **523**

DATE	DESCRIPTION	POST. REF.	DEBIT	CREDIT	BALANCE DEBIT	BALANCE CREDIT

Analyze:

Copyright © 2017 by McGraw-Hill Education. All rights reserved.

Name ______________________

PROBLEM 6.3A or 6.3B (continued)

GENERAL LEDGER

ACCOUNT ______________________ ACCOUNT NO. ________

DATE	DESCRIPTION	POST. REF.	DEBIT	CREDIT	BALANCE	
					DEBIT	CREDIT

ACCOUNT ______________________ ACCOUNT NO. ________

DATE	DESCRIPTION	POST. REF.	DEBIT	CREDIT	BALANCE	
					DEBIT	CREDIT

ACCOUNT ______________________ ACCOUNT NO. ________

DATE	DESCRIPTION	POST. REF.	DEBIT	CREDIT	BALANCE	
					DEBIT	CREDIT

ACCOUNT ______________________ ACCOUNT NO. ________

DATE	DESCRIPTION	POST. REF.	DEBIT	CREDIT	BALANCE	
					DEBIT	CREDIT

ACCOUNT ______________________ ACCOUNT NO. ________

DATE	DESCRIPTION	POST. REF.	DEBIT	CREDIT	BALANCE	
					DEBIT	CREDIT

Copyright © 2017 by McGraw-Hill Education. All rights reserved.

Name ______________________

PROBLEM 6.3A or 6.3B (continued)

GENERAL LEDGER

ACCOUNT ______________________ ACCOUNT NO. ________

DATE		DESCRIPTION	POST. REF.	DEBIT	CREDIT	BALANCE	
						DEBIT	CREDIT

ACCOUNT ______________________ ACCOUNT NO. ________

DATE		DESCRIPTION	POST. REF.	DEBIT	CREDIT	BALANCE	
						DEBIT	CREDIT

ACCOUNT ______________________ ACCOUNT NO. ________

DATE		DESCRIPTION	POST. REF.	DEBIT	CREDIT	BALANCE	
						DEBIT	CREDIT

ACCOUNT ______________________ ACCOUNT NO. ________

DATE		DESCRIPTION	POST. REF.	DEBIT	CREDIT	BALANCE	
						DEBIT	CREDIT

ACCOUNT ______________________ ACCOUNT NO. ________

DATE		DESCRIPTION	POST. REF.	DEBIT	CREDIT	BALANCE	
						DEBIT	CREDIT

Copyright © 2017 by McGraw-Hill Education. All rights reserved.

Name

PROBLEM 6.4A or 6.4B

	ACCOUNT NAME	TRIAL BALANCE		ADJUSTMENTS	
		DEBIT	CREDIT	DEBIT	CREDIT
1					
2					
3					
4					
5					
6					
7					
8					
9					
10					
11					
12					
13					
14					
15					
16					
17					
18					
19					
20					
21					
22					
23					
24					
25					
26					
27					
28					
29					
30					
31					
32					

Copyright © 2017 by McGraw-Hill Education. All rights reserved.

Name

PROBLEM 6.4A or 6.4B (continued)

ADJUSTED TRIAL BALANCE		INCOME STATEMENT		BALANCE SHEET		
DEBIT	CREDIT	DEBIT	CREDIT	DEBIT	CREDIT	
						1
						2
						3
						4
						5
						6
						7
						8
						9
						10
						11
						12
						13
						14
						15
						16
						17
						18
						19
						20
						21
						22
						23
						24
						25
						26
						27
						28
						29
						30
						31
						32

Copyright © 2017 by McGraw-Hill Education. All rights reserved.

Name ______________________________

PROBLEM 6.4A or 6.4B (continued)

GENERAL JOURNAL PAGE______

	DATE		DESCRIPTION	POST. REF.	DEBIT	CREDIT	
1							1
2							2
3							3
4							4
5							5
6							6
7							7
8							8
9							9
10							10
11							11
12							12
13							13

GENERAL JOURNAL PAGE______

	DATE		DESCRIPTION	POST. REF.	DEBIT	CREDIT	
1							1
2							2
3							3
4							4
5							5
6							6
7							7
8							8
9							9
10							10
11							11
12							12
13							13
14							14
15							15
16							16
17							17
18							18

Copyright © 2017 by McGraw-Hill Education. All rights reserved.

Name

PROBLEM 6.4A or 6.4B (continued)

GENERAL LEDGER

ACCOUNT **Supplies** ACCOUNT NO. **121**

DATE	DESCRIPTION	POST. REF.	DEBIT	CREDIT	BALANCE DEBIT	BALANCE CREDIT

ACCOUNT **Prepaid Advertising** ACCOUNT NO. **131**

DATE	DESCRIPTION	POST. REF.	DEBIT	CREDIT	BALANCE DEBIT	BALANCE CREDIT

ACCOUNT **Accumulated Depreciation—** ACCOUNT NO. **142**

DATE	DESCRIPTION	POST. REF.	DEBIT	CREDIT	BALANCE DEBIT	BALANCE CREDIT

ACCOUNT **Capital** ACCOUNT NO. **301**

DATE	DESCRIPTION	POST. REF.	DEBIT	CREDIT	BALANCE DEBIT	BALANCE CREDIT

ACCOUNT **Drawing** ACCOUNT NO. **302**

DATE	DESCRIPTION	POST. REF.	DEBIT	CREDIT	BALANCE DEBIT	BALANCE CREDIT

Copyright © 2017 by McGraw-Hill Education. All rights reserved.

Name ____________________

PROBLEM 6.4A or 6.4B (continued)

GENERAL LEDGER

ACCOUNT **Income Summary** ACCOUNT NO. **399**

DATE	DESCRIPTION	POST. REF.	DEBIT	CREDIT	BALANCE DEBIT	BALANCE CREDIT

ACCOUNT **Fees Income** ACCOUNT NO. **401**

DATE	DESCRIPTION	POST. REF.	DEBIT	CREDIT	BALANCE DEBIT	BALANCE CREDIT

GENERAL LEDGER

ACCOUNT **Salaries Expense** ACCOUNT NO. **511**

DATE	DESCRIPTION	POST. REF.	DEBIT	CREDIT	BALANCE DEBIT	BALANCE CREDIT

ACCOUNT **Utilities Expense** ACCOUNT NO. **514**

DATE	DESCRIPTION	POST. REF.	DEBIT	CREDIT	BALANCE DEBIT	BALANCE CREDIT

ACCOUNT **Supplies Expense** ACCOUNT NO. **517**

DATE	DESCRIPTION	POST. REF.	DEBIT	CREDIT	BALANCE DEBIT	BALANCE CREDIT

Copyright © 2017 by McGraw-Hill Education. All rights reserved.

Name

PROBLEM 6.4A or 6.4B (continued)

ACCOUNT **Depreciation Expense—** ACCOUNT NO. **523**

DATE		DESCRIPTION	POST. REF.	DEBIT	CREDIT	BALANCE DEBIT	BALANCE CREDIT

ACCOUNT **Advertising Expense** ACCOUNT NO. **526**

DATE		DESCRIPTION	POST. REF.	DEBIT	CREDIT	BALANCE DEBIT	BALANCE CREDIT

ACCOUNT NAME	DEBIT	CREDIT

Analyze:

Copyright © 2017 by McGraw-Hill Education. All rights reserved.

Name

CRITICAL THINKING PROBLEM 6.1

Contemporary Fashions
Worksheet
Month Ended December 31, 2019

	ACCOUNT NAME	TRIAL BALANCE DEBIT	TRIAL BALANCE CREDIT	ADJUSTMENTS DEBIT	ADJUSTMENTS CREDIT
1	Cash	40 800 00			
2	Accounts Receivable	9 000 00			
3	Supplies	7 200 00			(a) 3 600 00
4	Prepaid Insurance	10 800 00			(b) 2 400 00
5	Machinery	84 000 00			
6	Accumulated Depreciation—Machinery				(c) 1 200 00
7	Accounts Payable		27 000 00		
8	Helen Kennedy, Capital		149 160 00		
9	Helen Kennedy, Drawing	6 000 00			
10	Fees Income		165 000 00		
11	Supplies Expense			(a) 3 600 00	
12	Insurance Expense			(b) 2 400 00	
13	Salaries Expense	11 100 00			
14	Depreciation Expense—Machinery			(c) 1 200 00	
15	Utilities Expense	1 680 00			
16	Totals	170 580 00	170 580 00	7 200 00	7 200 00
17	Net Income				
18					
19					
20					
21					
22					
23					
24					
25					
26					
27					
28					
29					
30					
31					
32					

Copyright © 2017 by McGraw-Hill Education. All rights reserved.

CRITICAL THINKING PROBLEM 6.1 (continued)

	ADJUSTED TRIAL BALANCE		INCOME STATEMENT		BALANCE SHEET		
	DEBIT	CREDIT	DEBIT	CREDIT	DEBIT	CREDIT	
							1
							2
							3
							4
							5
							6
							7
							8
							9
							10
							11
							12
							13
							14
							15
							16
							17
							18
							19
							20
							21
							22
							23
							24
							25
							26
							27
							28
							29
							30
							31
							32

Copyright © 2017 by McGraw-Hill Education. All rights reserved.

Name

CRITICAL THINKING PROBLEM 6.1 (continued)

Copyright © 2017 by McGraw-Hill Education. All rights reserved.

Name

CRITICAL THINKING PROBLEM 6.1 (continued)

GENERAL JOURNAL PAGE

	DATE		DESCRIPTION	POST. REF.	DEBIT	CREDIT	
1							1
2							2
3							3
4							4
5							5
6							6
7							7
8							8
9							9
10							10
11							11
12							12
13							13
14							14
15							15
16							16

Copyright © 2017 by McGraw-Hill Education. All rights reserved.

Name

CRITICAL THINKING PROBLEM 6.1 (continued)

GENERAL JOURNAL PAGE

	DATE		DESCRIPTION	POST. REF.	DEBIT	CREDIT	
1							1
2							2
3							3
4							4
5							5
6							6
7							7
8							8
9							9
10							10
11							11
12							12
13							13
14							14
15							15
16							16
17							17
18							18

ACCOUNT NAME	DEBIT	CREDIT

Analyze:

Copyright © 2017 by McGraw-Hill Education. All rights reserved.

Name

CRITICAL THINKING PROBLEM 6.2

1.

2.

GENERAL JOURNAL

PAGE

	DATE		DESCRIPTION	POST. REF.	DEBIT	CREDIT	
1							1
2							2
3							3
4							4
5							5
6							6

3.

Copyright © 2017 by McGraw-Hill Education. All rights reserved.

Name

CRITICAL THINKING PROBLEM 6.2 (continued)

Copyright © 2017 by McGraw-Hill Education. All rights reserved.

MINI-PRACTICE SET 1

Name ______________________

Service Business Accounting Cycle

GENERAL JOURNAL

PAGE ________

DATE		DESCRIPTION	POST. REF.	DEBIT	CREDIT

Copyright © 2017 by McGraw-Hill Education. All rights reserved.

Name ______________________

GENERAL JOURNAL

PAGE ________

DATE	DESCRIPTION	POST. REF.	DEBIT	CREDIT

Copyright © 2017 by McGraw-Hill Education. All rights reserved.

Name ______________________

GENERAL JOURNAL

PAGE ________

	DATE	DESCRIPTION	POST. REF.	DEBIT	CREDIT	
1						1
2						2
3						3
4						4
5						5
6						6
7						7
8						8
9						9
10						10
11						11
12						12
13						13
14						14
15						15
16						16
17						17
18						18
19						19
20						20
21						21
22						22
23						23
24						24
25						25
26						26
27						27
28						28
29						29
30						30
31						31
32						32
33						33
34						34
35						35
36						36
37						37
38						38
39						39

Copyright © 2017 by McGraw-Hill Education. All rights reserved.

 Name ____________

GENERAL JOURNAL PAGE____

	DATE	DESCRIPTION	POST. REF.	DEBIT	CREDIT	
1						1
2						2
3						3
4						4
5						5
6						6
7						7
8						8
9						9
10						10
11						11
12						12
13						13
14						14
15						15
16						16
17						17
18						18
19						19
20						20
21						21
22						22
23						23
24						24
25						25
26						26
27						27
28						28
29						29
30						30
31						31
32						32
33						33
34						34
35						35
36						36
37						37
38						38
39						39

Copyright © 2017 by McGraw-Hill Education. All rights reserved.

 Name ____________________

GENERAL LEDGER

ACCOUNT ____________________ ACCOUNT NO. __________

DATE	DESCRIPTION	POST. REF.	DEBIT	CREDIT	BALANCE	
					DEBIT	CREDIT

ACCOUNT ____________________ ACCOUNT NO. __________

DATE	DESCRIPTION	POST. REF.	DEBIT	CREDIT	BALANCE	
					DEBIT	CREDIT

Copyright © 2017 by McGraw-Hill Education. All rights reserved.

 Name ______________________

GENERAL LEDGER

ACCOUNT ______________________ ACCOUNT NO. ________

DATE		DESCRIPTION	POST. REF.	DEBIT	CREDIT	BALANCE	
						DEBIT	CREDIT

ACCOUNT ______________________ ACCOUNT NO. ________

DATE		DESCRIPTION	POST. REF.	DEBIT	CREDIT	BALANCE	
						DEBIT	CREDIT

ACCOUNT ______________________ ACCOUNT NO. ________

DATE		DESCRIPTION	POST. REF.	DEBIT	CREDIT	BALANCE	
						DEBIT	CREDIT

ACCOUNT ______________________ ACCOUNT NO. ________

DATE		DESCRIPTION	POST. REF.	DEBIT	CREDIT	BALANCE	
						DEBIT	CREDIT

ACCOUNT ______________________ ACCOUNT NO. ________

DATE		DESCRIPTION	POST. REF.	DEBIT	CREDIT	BALANCE	
						DEBIT	CREDIT

Copyright © 2017 by McGraw-Hill Education. All rights reserved.

Name ____________________

GENERAL LEDGER

ACCOUNT ____________________ ACCOUNT NO. ________

DATE		DESCRIPTION	POST. REF.	DEBIT	CREDIT	BALANCE DEBIT	BALANCE CREDIT

ACCOUNT ____________________ ACCOUNT NO. ________

DATE		DESCRIPTION	POST. REF.	DEBIT	CREDIT	BALANCE DEBIT	BALANCE CREDIT

ACCOUNT ____________________ ACCOUNT NO. ________

DATE		DESCRIPTION	POST. REF.	DEBIT	CREDIT	BALANCE DEBIT	BALANCE CREDIT

ACCOUNT ____________________ ACCOUNT NO. ________

DATE		DESCRIPTION	POST. REF.	DEBIT	CREDIT	BALANCE DEBIT	BALANCE CREDIT

Copyright © 2017 by McGraw-Hill Education. All rights reserved.

 Name ______________________________

GENERAL LEDGER

ACCOUNT ______________________________ ACCOUNT NO. __________

DATE		DESCRIPTION	POST. REF.	DEBIT	CREDIT	BALANCE DEBIT	BALANCE CREDIT

ACCOUNT ______________________________ ACCOUNT NO. __________

DATE		DESCRIPTION	POST. REF.	DEBIT	CREDIT	BALANCE DEBIT	BALANCE CREDIT

ACCOUNT ______________________________ ACCOUNT NO. __________

DATE		DESCRIPTION	POST. REF.	DEBIT	CREDIT	BALANCE DEBIT	BALANCE CREDIT

ACCOUNT ______________________________ ACCOUNT NO. __________

DATE		DESCRIPTION	POST. REF.	DEBIT	CREDIT	BALANCE DEBIT	BALANCE CREDIT

ACCOUNT ______________________________ ACCOUNT NO. __________

DATE		DESCRIPTION	POST. REF.	DEBIT	CREDIT	BALANCE DEBIT	BALANCE CREDIT

Copyright © 2017 by McGraw-Hill Education. All rights reserved.

 Name ______________________

GENERAL LEDGER

ACCOUNT ______________________ ACCOUNT NO. ________

DATE		DESCRIPTION	POST. REF.	DEBIT	CREDIT	BALANCE DEBIT	BALANCE CREDIT

ACCOUNT ______________________ ACCOUNT NO. ________

DATE		DESCRIPTION	POST. REF.	DEBIT	CREDIT	BALANCE DEBIT	BALANCE CREDIT

ACCOUNT ______________________ ACCOUNT NO. ________

DATE		DESCRIPTION	POST. REF.	DEBIT	CREDIT	BALANCE DEBIT	BALANCE CREDIT

ACCOUNT ______________________ ACCOUNT NO. ________

DATE		DESCRIPTION	POST. REF.	DEBIT	CREDIT	BALANCE DEBIT	BALANCE CREDIT

ACCOUNT ______________________ ACCOUNT NO. ________

DATE		DESCRIPTION	POST. REF.	DEBIT	CREDIT	BALANCE DEBIT	BALANCE CREDIT

Copyright © 2017 by McGraw-Hill Education. All rights reserved.

MINI-PRACTICE SET 1 (continued)

Name ______________________

	ACCOUNT NAME	TRIAL BALANCE		ADJUSTMENTS	
		DEBIT	CREDIT	DEBIT	CREDIT
1					
2					
3					
4					
5					
6					
7					
8					
9					
10					
11					
12					
13					
14					
15					
16					
17					
18					
19					
20					
21					
22					
23					
24					
25					
26					
27					
28					
29					
30					
31					
32					
33					
34					
35					
36					
37					

Copyright © 2017 by McGraw-Hill Education. All rights reserved.

 Name ______________________

ADJUSTED TRIAL BALANCE		INCOME STATEMENT		BALANCE SHEET		
DEBIT	CREDIT	DEBIT	CREDIT	DEBIT	CREDIT	
						1
						2
						3
						4
						5
						6
						7
						8
						9
						10
						11
						12
						13
						14
						15
						16
						17
						18
						19
						20
						21
						22
						23
						24
						25
						26
						27
						28
						29
						30
						31
						32
						33
						34
						35
						36
						37

Copyright © 2017 by McGraw-Hill Education. All rights reserved.

 Name

Copyright © 2017 by McGraw-Hill Education. All rights reserved.

 Name

ACCOUNT NAME	DEBIT	CREDIT

 Copyright © 2017 by McGraw-Hill Education. All rights reserved.

MINI-PRACTICE SET 1 (continued)

Name

Analyze:

Copyright © 2017 by McGraw-Hill Education. All rights reserved.

WORKING PAPERS

Name ______________________

EXERCISE 7.1

1. ______________________
2. ______________________
3. ______________________
4. ______________________
5. ______________________
6. ______________________
7. ______________________
8. ______________________

EXERCISE 7.2

	Dr.	Cr.
1.		
2.		
3.		
4.		
5.		
6.		

EXERCISE 7.3

SALES JOURNAL

PAGE ______

	DATE	SALES SLIP NO.	CUSTOMER'S NAME	POST. REF.	ACCOUNTS RECEIVABLE DEBIT	SALES TAX PAYABLE CREDIT	SALES CREDIT	
1								1
2								2
3								3
4								4
5								5

Copyright © 2017 by McGraw-Hill Education. All rights reserved.

Name ______________________

EXERCISE 7.4

GENERAL JOURNAL PAGE ______

	DATE		DESCRIPTION	POST. REF.	DEBIT	CREDIT	
1							1
2							2
3							3
4							4
5							5
6							6
7							7
8							8
9							9
10							10
11							11
12							12
13							13
14							14
15							15

EXERCISE 7.5

1. ______________________

2. ______________________

3. ______________________

4. ______________________

EXERCISE 7.6

1. ______________________
2. ______________________
3. ______________________

Copyright © 2017 by McGraw-Hill Education. All rights reserved.

Name

EXERCISE 7.7

1.
2.
3.

EXERCISE 7.8

GENERAL JOURNAL PAGE

	DATE		DESCRIPTION	POST. REF.	DEBIT	CREDIT	
1							1
2							2
3							3
4							4
5							5

EXERCISE 7.9

Balance of Accounts Receivable:

Copyright © 2017 by McGraw-Hill Education. All rights reserved.

Name ________________

EXERCISE 7.10

GENERAL LEDGER

ACCOUNT ________________ ACCOUNT NO. ________

DATE		DESCRIPTION	POST. REF.	DEBIT	CREDIT	BALANCE	
						DEBIT	CREDIT

ACCOUNT ________________ ACCOUNT NO. ________

DATE		DESCRIPTION	POST. REF.	DEBIT	CREDIT	BALANCE	
						DEBIT	CREDIT

ACCOUNT ________________ ACCOUNT NO. ________

DATE		DESCRIPTION	POST. REF.	DEBIT	CREDIT	BALANCE	
						DEBIT	CREDIT

ACCOUNTS RECEIVABLE SUBSIDIARY LEDGER

NAME ________________ TERMS ________

DATE		DESCRIPTION	POST. REF.	DEBIT	CREDIT	BALANCE

NAME ________________ TERMS ________

DATE		DESCRIPTION	POST. REF.	DEBIT	CREDIT	BALANCE

Copyright © 2017 by McGraw-Hill Education. All rights reserved.

Name

PROBLEM 7.1A or 7.1B

SALES JOURNAL PAGE

	DATE	SALES SLIP NO.	CUSTOMER'S NAME	POST. REF.	ACCOUNTS RECEIVABLE DEBIT	SALES TAX PAYABLE CREDIT	SALES CREDIT	
1								1
2								2
3								3
4								4
5								5
6								6
7								7
8								8
9								9
10								10
11								11
12								12

GENERAL LEDGER

ACCOUNT ACCOUNT NO.

DATE	DESCRIPTION	POST. REF.	DEBIT	CREDIT	BALANCE	
					DEBIT	CREDIT

ACCOUNT ACCOUNT NO.

DATE	DESCRIPTION	POST. REF.	DEBIT	CREDIT	BALANCE	
					DEBIT	CREDIT

ACCOUNT ACCOUNT NO.

DATE	DESCRIPTION	POST. REF.	DEBIT	CREDIT	BALANCE	
					DEBIT	CREDIT

Analyze:

Copyright © 2017 by McGraw-Hill Education. All rights reserved.

Name ____________________

PROBLEM 7.2A or 7.2B

SALES JOURNAL PAGE______

	DATE		SALES SLIP NO.	CUSTOMER'S NAME	POST. REF.	ACCOUNTS RECEIVABLE DEBIT	SALES TAX PAYABLE CREDIT	SALES CREDIT	
1									1
2									2
3									3
4									4
5									5
6									6
7									7
8									8
9									9
10									10
11									11
12									12

GENERAL JOURNAL PAGE______

	DATE		DESCRIPTION	POST. REF.	DEBIT	CREDIT	
1							1
2							2
3							3
4							4
5							5
6							6
7							7
8							8
9							9
10							10
11							11
12							12
13							13
14							14
15							15
16							16
17							17
18							18
19							19
20							20
21							21

Copyright © 2017 by McGraw-Hill Education. All rights reserved.

Name ____________________

PROBLEM 7.2A or 7.2B (continued)

GENERAL LEDGER

ACCOUNT ____________________ ACCOUNT NO. ________

DATE	DESCRIPTION	POST. REF.	DEBIT	CREDIT	BALANCE DEBIT	BALANCE CREDIT

ACCOUNT ____________________ ACCOUNT NO. ________

DATE	DESCRIPTION	POST. REF.	DEBIT	CREDIT	BALANCE DEBIT	BALANCE CREDIT

ACCOUNT ____________________ ACCOUNT NO. ________

DATE	DESCRIPTION	POST. REF.	DEBIT	CREDIT	BALANCE DEBIT	BALANCE CREDIT

ACCOUNT ____________________ ACCOUNT NO. ________

DATE	DESCRIPTION	POST. REF.	DEBIT	CREDIT	BALANCE DEBIT	BALANCE CREDIT

Copyright © 2017 by McGraw-Hill Education. All rights reserved.

Name

PROBLEM 7.2A or 7.2B (continued)

Analyze:

PROBLEM 7.3A or 7.3B

SALES JOURNAL

PAGE

	DATE	SALES SLIP NO.	CUSTOMER'S NAME	POST. REF.	ACCOUNTS RECEIVABLE DEBIT	SALES TAX PAYABLE CREDIT	SALES CREDIT	
1								1
2								2
3								3
4								4
5								5
6								6
7								7
8								8
9								9
10								10
11								11
12								12

Copyright © 2017 by McGraw-Hill Education. All rights reserved.

Name

PROBLEM 7.3A or 7.3B (continued)

GENERAL JOURNAL

PAGE

	DATE		DESCRIPTION	POST. REF.	DEBIT	CREDIT	
1							1
2							2
3							3
4							4
5							5
6							6
7							7
8							8
9							9
10							10
11							11
12							12
13							13
14							14
15							15

GENERAL LEDGER

ACCOUNT ______ ACCOUNT NO. ______

DATE		DESCRIPTION	POST. REF.	DEBIT	CREDIT	BALANCE	
						DEBIT	CREDIT

ACCOUNT ______ ACCOUNT NO. ______

DATE		DESCRIPTION	POST. REF.	DEBIT	CREDIT	BALANCE	
						DEBIT	CREDIT

Copyright © 2017 by McGraw-Hill Education. All rights reserved.

Name ______________________________

PROBLEM 7.3A or 7.3B (continued)

GENERAL LEDGER

ACCOUNT ______________________________ ACCOUNT NO. __________

DATE		DESCRIPTION	POST. REF.	DEBIT	CREDIT	BALANCE DEBIT	BALANCE CREDIT

ACCOUNT ______________________________ ACCOUNT NO. __________

DATE		DESCRIPTION	POST. REF.	DEBIT	CREDIT	BALANCE DEBIT	BALANCE CREDIT

ACCOUNTS RECEIVABLE SUBSIDIARY LEDGER

NAME ______________________________ TERMS __________

DATE		DESCRIPTION	POST. REF.	DEBIT	CREDIT	BALANCE

NAME ______________________________ TERMS __________

DATE		DESCRIPTION	POST. REF.	DEBIT	CREDIT	BALANCE

NAME ______________________________ TERMS __________

DATE		DESCRIPTION	POST. REF.	DEBIT	CREDIT	BALANCE

Copyright © 2017 by McGraw-Hill Education. All rights reserved.

Name

PROBLEM 7.3A or 7.3B (continued)

ACCOUNTS RECEIVABLE SUBSIDIARY LEDGER

NAME ______ TERMS ______

DATE		DESCRIPTION	POST. REF.	DEBIT	CREDIT	BALANCE

NAME ______ TERMS ______

DATE		DESCRIPTION	POST. REF.	DEBIT	CREDIT	BALANCE

NAME ______ TERMS ______

DATE		DESCRIPTION	POST. REF.	DEBIT	CREDIT	BALANCE

NAME ______ TERMS ______

DATE		DESCRIPTION	POST. REF.	DEBIT	CREDIT	BALANCE

NAME ______ TERMS ______

DATE		DESCRIPTION	POST. REF.	DEBIT	CREDIT	BALANCE

NAME ______ TERMS ______

DATE		DESCRIPTION	POST. REF.	DEBIT	CREDIT	BALANCE

Copyright © 2017 by McGraw-Hill Education. All rights reserved.

Name

PROBLEM 7.3A or 7.3B (continued)

Balance of Accounts Receivable account: ____________

Analyze: ______________________________

PROBLEM 7.4A or 7.4B

SALES JOURNAL PAGE______

	DATE		SALES SLIP NO.	CUSTOMER'S NAME	POST. REF.	ACCOUNTS RECEIVABLE DR./ SALES CR.	
1							1
2							2
3							3
4							4
5							5
6							6
7							7
8							8
9							9
10							10
11							11
12							12

Copyright © 2017 by McGraw-Hill Education. All rights reserved.

Name

PROBLEM 7.4A or 7.4B (continued)

GENERAL JOURNAL

PAGE

	DATE		DESCRIPTION	POST. REF.	DEBIT	CREDIT	
1							1
2							2
3							3
4							4
5							5
6							6
7							7
8							8
9							9
10							10
11							11
12							12
13							13

GENERAL LEDGER

ACCOUNT ACCOUNT NO.

DATE		DESCRIPTION	POST. REF.	DEBIT	CREDIT	BALANCE	
						DEBIT	CREDIT

ACCOUNT ACCOUNT NO.

DATE		DESCRIPTION	POST. REF.	DEBIT	CREDIT	BALANCE	
						DEBIT	CREDIT

ACCOUNT ACCOUNT NO.

DATE		DESCRIPTION	POST. REF.	DEBIT	CREDIT	BALANCE	
						DEBIT	CREDIT

Copyright © 2017 by McGraw-Hill Education. All rights reserved.

Name ______________________

PROBLEM 7.4A or 7.4B (continued)

ACCOUNTS RECEIVABLE SUBSIDIARY LEDGER

NAME ______________________ TERMS __________

DATE		DESCRIPTION	POST. REF.	DEBIT	CREDIT	BALANCE

NAME ______________________ TERMS __________

DATE		DESCRIPTION	POST. REF.	DEBIT	CREDIT	BALANCE

NAME ______________________ TERMS __________

DATE		DESCRIPTION	POST. REF.	DEBIT	CREDIT	BALANCE

NAME ______________________ TERMS __________

DATE		DESCRIPTION	POST. REF.	DEBIT	CREDIT	BALANCE

NAME ______________________ TERMS __________

DATE		DESCRIPTION	POST. REF.	DEBIT	CREDIT	BALANCE

Copyright © 2017 by McGraw-Hill Education. All rights reserved.

Name

PROBLEM 7.4A or 7.4B (continued)

ACCOUNTS RECEIVABLE SUBSIDIARY LEDGER

NAME ______ TERMS ______

DATE		DESCRIPTION	POST. REF.	DEBIT	CREDIT	BALANCE

Balance of Accounts Receivable account: ______

Analyze: ______

CRITICAL THINKING PROBLEM 7.1

SALES JOURNAL

PAGE ______

	DATE		SALES SLIP NO.	CUSTOMER'S NAME	POST. REF.	ACCOUNTS RECEIVABLE DR./ SALES CR.	
1							1
2							2
3							3
4							4
5							5
6							6
7							7
8							8
9							9
10							10
11							11

Copyright © 2017 by McGraw-Hill Education. All rights reserved.

Name ______________________________

CRITICAL THINKING PROBLEM 7.1 (continued)

GENERAL JOURNAL PAGE_______

	DATE		DESCRIPTION	POST. REF.	DEBIT	CREDIT	
1							1
2							2
3							3
4							4
5							5
6							6
7							7

GENERAL LEDGER

ACCOUNT ______________________ ACCOUNT NO. ________

DATE		DESCRIPTION	POST. REF.	DEBIT	CREDIT	BALANCE	
						DEBIT	CREDIT

ACCOUNT ______________________ ACCOUNT NO. ________

DATE		DESCRIPTION	POST. REF.	DEBIT	CREDIT	BALANCE	
						DEBIT	CREDIT

ACCOUNT ______________________ ACCOUNT NO. ________

DATE		DESCRIPTION	POST. REF.	DEBIT	CREDIT	BALANCE	
						DEBIT	CREDIT

Copyright © 2017 by McGraw-Hill Education. All rights reserved.

Name

CRITICAL THINKING PROBLEM 7.1 (continued)

ACCOUNTS RECEIVABLE LEDGER

NAME ______________________ TERMS __________

DATE		DESCRIPTION	POST. REF.	DEBIT	CREDIT	BALANCE

NAME ______________________ TERMS __________

DATE		DESCRIPTION	POST. REF.	DEBIT	CREDIT	BALANCE

NAME ______________________ TERMS __________

DATE		DESCRIPTION	POST. REF.	DEBIT	CREDIT	BALANCE

NAME ______________________ TERMS __________

DATE		DESCRIPTION	POST. REF.	DEBIT	CREDIT	BALANCE

NAME ______________________ TERMS __________

DATE		DESCRIPTION	POST. REF.	DEBIT	CREDIT	BALANCE

Copyright © 2017 by McGraw-Hill Education. All rights reserved.

Name

CRITICAL THINKING PROBLEM 7.1 (continued)

ACCOUNTS RECEIVABLE SUBSIDIARY LEDGER

NAME ______________________ TERMS __________

DATE		DESCRIPTION	POST. REF.	DEBIT	CREDIT	BALANCE

Balance of Accounts Receivable account: __________

Analyze: ______________________

Copyright © 2017 by McGraw-Hill Education. All rights reserved.

Name

CRITICAL THINKING PROBLEM 7.2

1.

2.

3.

4.

Copyright © 2017 by McGraw-Hill Education. All rights reserved.

WORKING PAPERS

Name ______________________________

EXERCISE 8.1

1. ______________________
2. ______________________
3. ______________________
4. ______________________
5. ______________________
6. ______________________

EXERCISE 8.2

	Dr.	Cr.
1.		
2.		
3.		
4.		
5.		
6.		

EXERCISE 8.3

PURCHASES JOURNAL PAGE______

DATE		PURCHASED FROM	INVOICE NUMBER	INVOICE DATE	TERMS	POST. REF.	ACCOUNTS PAYABLE CREDIT	PURCHASES DEBIT	FREIGHT IN DEBIT

EXERCISE 8.4

GENERAL JOURNAL PAGE______

	DATE		DESCRIPTION	POST. REF.	DEBIT	CREDIT	
1							1
2							2
3							3
4							4
5							5
6							6
7							7
8							8
9							9
10							10

Copyright © 2017 by McGraw-Hill Education. All rights reserved.

Name ____________________

EXERCISE 8.5

GENERAL JOURNAL PAGE ______

	DATE		DESCRIPTION	POST. REF.	DEBIT	CREDIT	
1							1
2							2
3							3
4							4
5							5
6							6
7							7

EXERCISE 8.6

EXERCISE 8.7

a. ____________________

b. ____________________

c. ____________________

d. ____________________

EXERCISE 8.8

a. ____________________

b. ____________________

c. ____________________

d. ____________________

Copyright © 2017 by McGraw-Hill Education. All rights reserved.

Name ____________________

PROBLEM 8.1A or 8.1B

PURCHASES JOURNAL

PAGE ________

DATE		PURCHASED FROM	INVOICE NUMBER	INVOICE DATE	TERMS	POST. REF.	ACCOUNTS PAYABLE CREDIT	PURCHASES DEBIT	FREIGHT IN DEBIT

GENERAL JOURNAL

PAGE ________

	DATE		DESCRIPTION	POST. REF.	DEBIT	CREDIT	
1							1
2							2
3							3
4							4
5							5
6							6
7							7
8							8
9							9
10							10
11							11
12							12
13							13
14							14
15							15
16							16
17							17
18							18
19							19

Copyright © 2017 by McGraw-Hill Education. All rights reserved.

Name ______________________

PROBLEM 8.1A or 8.1B (continued)

GENERAL LEDGER

ACCOUNT ______________________ ACCOUNT NO. ________

DATE		DESCRIPTION	POST. REF.	DEBIT	CREDIT	BALANCE DEBIT	BALANCE CREDIT

ACCOUNT ______________________ ACCOUNT NO. ________

DATE		DESCRIPTION	POST. REF.	DEBIT	CREDIT	BALANCE DEBIT	BALANCE CREDIT

ACCOUNT ______________________ ACCOUNT NO. ________

DATE		DESCRIPTION	POST. REF.	DEBIT	CREDIT	BALANCE DEBIT	BALANCE CREDIT

ACCOUNT ______________________ ACCOUNT NO. ________

DATE		DESCRIPTION	POST. REF.	DEBIT	CREDIT	BALANCE DEBIT	BALANCE CREDIT

Analyze: ______________________

Copyright © 2017 by McGraw-Hill Education. All rights reserved.

Name ______________________________

PROBLEM 8.2A or 8.2B

ACCOUNTS PAYABLE SUBSIDIARY LEDGER

NAME ______________________________ TERMS __________

DATE		DESCRIPTION	POST. REF.	DEBIT	CREDIT	BALANCE

NAME ______________________________ TERMS __________

DATE		DESCRIPTION	POST. REF.	DEBIT	CREDIT	BALANCE

NAME ______________________________ TERMS __________

DATE		DESCRIPTION	POST. REF.	DEBIT	CREDIT	BALANCE

NAME ______________________________ TERMS __________

DATE		DESCRIPTION	POST. REF.	DEBIT	CREDIT	BALANCE

NAME ______________________________ TERMS __________

DATE		DESCRIPTION	POST. REF.	DEBIT	CREDIT	BALANCE

Copyright © 2017 by McGraw-Hill Education. All rights reserved.

Name

PROBLEM 8.2A or 8.2B (continued)

Analyze:

EXTRA FORM

Copyright © 2017 by McGraw-Hill Education. All rights reserved.

Name

PROBLEM 8.3A or 8.3B

PURCHASES JOURNAL

PAGE

DATE		PURCHASED FROM	INVOICE NUMBER	INVOICE DATE	TERMS	POST. REF.	ACCOUNTS PAYABLE CREDIT	PURCHASES DEBIT	FREIGHT IN DEBIT

GENERAL JOURNAL

PAGE

	DATE		DESCRIPTION	POST. REF.	DEBIT	CREDIT	
1							1
2							2
3							3
4							4
5							5
6							6
7							7
8							8
9							9
10							10
11							11
12							12
13							13
14							14
15							15

Copyright © 2017 by McGraw-Hill Education. All rights reserved.

Name ______________________________

PROBLEM 8.3A or 8.3B (continued)

GENERAL LEDGER

ACCOUNT ______________________ ACCOUNT NO. ________

DATE	DESCRIPTION	POST. REF.	DEBIT	CREDIT	BALANCE DEBIT	BALANCE CREDIT

ACCOUNT ______________________ ACCOUNT NO. ________

DATE	DESCRIPTION	POST. REF.	DEBIT	CREDIT	BALANCE DEBIT	BALANCE CREDIT

ACCOUNT ______________________ ACCOUNT NO. ________

DATE	DESCRIPTION	POST. REF.	DEBIT	CREDIT	BALANCE DEBIT	BALANCE CREDIT

ACCOUNT ______________________ ACCOUNT NO. ________

DATE	DESCRIPTION	POST. REF.	DEBIT	CREDIT	BALANCE DEBIT	BALANCE CREDIT

Copyright © 2017 by McGraw-Hill Education. All rights reserved.

Name ____________________

PROBLEM 8.3A or 8.3B (continued)

ACCOUNTS PAYABLE SUBSIDIARY LEDGER

NAME ____________________ TERMS __________

DATE		DESCRIPTION	POST. REF.	DEBIT	CREDIT	BALANCE

NAME ____________________ TERMS __________

DATE		DESCRIPTION	POST. REF.	DEBIT	CREDIT	BALANCE

NAME ____________________ TERMS __________

DATE		DESCRIPTION	POST. REF.	DEBIT	CREDIT	BALANCE

NAME ____________________ TERMS __________

DATE		DESCRIPTION	POST. REF.	DEBIT	CREDIT	BALANCE

NAME ____________________ TERMS __________

DATE		DESCRIPTION	POST. REF.	DEBIT	CREDIT	BALANCE

Copyright © 2017 by McGraw-Hill Education. All rights reserved.

Name

PROBLEM 8.3A or 8.3B (continued)

Analyze:

EXTRA FORMS

NAME _______________ TERMS _______________

DATE		DESCRIPTION	POST. REF.	DEBIT	CREDIT	BALANCE

NAME _______________ TERMS _______________

DATE		DESCRIPTION	POST. REF.	DEBIT	CREDIT	BALANCE

Copyright © 2017 by McGraw-Hill Education. All rights reserved.

Name

PROBLEM 8.4A or 8.4B

PURCHASES JOURNAL PAGE

DATE	PURCHASED FROM	INVOICE NUMBER	INVOICE DATE	TERMS	POST. REF.	ACCOUNTS PAYABLE CREDIT	PURCHASES DEBIT	FREIGHT IN DEBIT

GENERAL JOURNAL PAGE

	DATE	DESCRIPTION	POST. REF.	DEBIT	CREDIT	
1						1
2						2
3						3
4						4
5						5
6						6
7						7
8						8
9						9
10						10
11						11
12						12
13						13
14						14
15						15

Copyright © 2017 by McGraw-Hill Education. All rights reserved.

Name

PROBLEM 8.4A or 8.4B (continued)

GENERAL LEDGER

ACCOUNT ______ ACCOUNT NO. ______

DATE	DESCRIPTION	POST. REF.	DEBIT	CREDIT	BALANCE DEBIT	BALANCE CREDIT

ACCOUNT ______ ACCOUNT NO. ______

DATE	DESCRIPTION	POST. REF.	DEBIT	CREDIT	BALANCE DEBIT	BALANCE CREDIT

ACCOUNT ______ ACCOUNT NO. ______

DATE	DESCRIPTION	POST. REF.	DEBIT	CREDIT	BALANCE DEBIT	BALANCE CREDIT

ACCOUNT ______ ACCOUNT NO. ______

DATE	DESCRIPTION	POST. REF.	DEBIT	CREDIT	BALANCE DEBIT	BALANCE CREDIT

Net Delivered Cost of Purchases

Copyright © 2017 by McGraw-Hill Education. All rights reserved.

Name ____________________

PROBLEM 8.4A or 8.4B (continued)

ACCOUNTS PAYABLE SUBSIDIARY LEDGER

NAME ____________________ TERMS ____________

DATE		DESCRIPTION	POST. REF.	DEBIT	CREDIT	BALANCE

NAME ____________________ TERMS ____________

DATE		DESCRIPTION	POST. REF.	DEBIT	CREDIT	BALANCE

NAME ____________________ TERMS ____________

DATE		DESCRIPTION	POST. REF.	DEBIT	CREDIT	BALANCE

NAME ____________________ TERMS ____________

DATE		DESCRIPTION	POST. REF.	DEBIT	CREDIT	BALANCE

NAME ____________________ TERMS ____________

DATE		DESCRIPTION	POST. REF.	DEBIT	CREDIT	BALANCE

Copyright © 2017 by McGraw-Hill Education. All rights reserved.

Name

PROBLEM 8.4A or 8.4B (continued)

Analyze:

EXTRA FORM

Copyright © 2017 by McGraw-Hill Education. All rights reserved.

Name

CRITICAL THINKING PROBLEM 8.1

PURCHASES JOURNAL PAGE____

DATE		PURCHASED FROM	INVOICE NUMBER	INVOICE DATE	TERMS	POST. REF.	ACCOUNTS PAYABLE CREDIT	PURCHASES DEBIT	FREIGHT IN DEBIT

SALES JOURNAL PAGE____

	DATE		SALES SLIP NO.	CUSTOMER'S NAME	POST. REF.	ACCOUNTS RECEIVABLE DEBIT	SALES TAX PAYABLE CREDIT	SALES CREDIT	
1									1
2									2
3									3
4									4
5									5
6									6
7									7
8									8
9									9
10									10
11									11
12									12
13									13
14									14
15									15

Copyright © 2017 by McGraw-Hill Education. All rights reserved.

Name

CRITICAL THINKING PROBLEM 8.1 (continued)

ACCOUNTS PAYABLE SUBSIDIARY LEDGER

NAME ______ TERMS ______

DATE		DESCRIPTION	POST. REF.	DEBIT	CREDIT	BALANCE

NAME ______ TERMS ______

DATE		DESCRIPTION	POST. REF.	DEBIT	CREDIT	BALANCE

NAME ______ TERMS ______

DATE		DESCRIPTION	POST. REF.	DEBIT	CREDIT	BALANCE

NAME ______ TERMS ______

DATE		DESCRIPTION	POST. REF.	DEBIT	CREDIT	BALANCE

NAME ______ TERMS ______

DATE		DESCRIPTION	POST. REF.	DEBIT	CREDIT	BALANCE

NAME ______ TERMS ______

DATE		DESCRIPTION	POST. REF.	DEBIT	CREDIT	BALANCE

Copyright © 2017 by McGraw-Hill Education. All rights reserved.

Name

CRITICAL THINKING PROBLEM 8.1 (continued)

ACCOUNTS PAYABLE SUBSIDIARY LEDGER

NAME ______ TERMS ______

DATE		DESCRIPTION	POST. REF.	DEBIT	CREDIT	BALANCE

NAME ______ TERMS ______

DATE		DESCRIPTION	POST. REF.	DEBIT	CREDIT	BALANCE

ACCOUNTS RECEIVABLE SUBSIDIARY LEDGER

NAME ______ TERMS ______

DATE		DESCRIPTION	POST. REF.	DEBIT	CREDIT	BALANCE

NAME ______ TERMS ______

DATE		DESCRIPTION	POST. REF.	DEBIT	CREDIT	BALANCE

NAME ______ TERMS ______

DATE		DESCRIPTION	POST. REF.	DEBIT	CREDIT	BALANCE

Copyright © 2017 by McGraw-Hill Education. All rights reserved.

Name

CRITICAL THINKING PROBLEM 8.1 (continued)

ACCOUNTS RECEIVABLE SUBSIDIARY LEDGER

NAME TERMS

DATE		DESCRIPTION	POST. REF.	DEBIT	CREDIT	BALANCE

NAME TERMS

DATE		DESCRIPTION	POST. REF.	DEBIT	CREDIT	BALANCE

NAME TERMS

DATE		DESCRIPTION	POST. REF.	DEBIT	CREDIT	BALANCE

NAME TERMS

DATE		DESCRIPTION	POST. REF.	DEBIT	CREDIT	BALANCE

NAME TERMS

DATE		DESCRIPTION	POST. REF.	DEBIT	CREDIT	BALANCE

NAME TERMS

DATE		DESCRIPTION	POST. REF.	DEBIT	CREDIT	BALANCE

Copyright © 2017 by McGraw-Hill Education. All rights reserved.

Name

CRITICAL THINKING PROBLEM 8.1 (continued)

ACCOUNTS RECEIVABLE SUBSIDIARY LEDGER

NAME ______ TERMS ______

DATE		DESCRIPTION	POST. REF.	DEBIT	CREDIT	BALANCE

NAME ______ TERMS ______

DATE		DESCRIPTION	POST. REF.	DEBIT	CREDIT	BALANCE

GENERAL LEDGER

ACCOUNT ______ ACCOUNT NO. ______

DATE		DESCRIPTION	POST. REF.	DEBIT	CREDIT	BALANCE	
						DEBIT	CREDIT

ACCOUNT ______ ACCOUNT NO. ______

DATE		DESCRIPTION	POST. REF.	DEBIT	CREDIT	BALANCE	
						DEBIT	CREDIT

ACCOUNT ______ ACCOUNT NO. ______

DATE		DESCRIPTION	POST. REF.	DEBIT	CREDIT	BALANCE	
						DEBIT	CREDIT

ACCOUNT ______ ACCOUNT NO. ______

DATE		DESCRIPTION	POST. REF.	DEBIT	CREDIT	BALANCE	
						DEBIT	CREDIT

Copyright © 2017 by McGraw-Hill Education. All rights reserved.

Name

CRITICAL THINKING PROBLEM 8.1 (continued)

GENERAL LEDGER

ACCOUNT ______ ACCOUNT NO. ______

DATE		DESCRIPTION	POST. REF.	DEBIT	CREDIT	BALANCE DEBIT	BALANCE CREDIT

ACCOUNT ______ ACCOUNT NO. ______

DATE		DESCRIPTION	POST. REF.	DEBIT	CREDIT	BALANCE DEBIT	BALANCE CREDIT

Copyright © 2017 by McGraw-Hill Education. All rights reserved.

Name

CRITICAL THINKING PROBLEM 8.1 (continued)

Analyze:

Copyright © 2017 by McGraw-Hill Education. All rights reserved.

Name

CRITICAL THINKING PROBLEM 8.2

Copyright © 2017 by McGraw-Hill Education. All rights reserved.

WORKING PAPERS

Name ____________________

EXERCISES 9.1, 9.2

EXERCISE 9.1

CASH RECEIPTS JOURNAL

PAGE____

DATE	DESCRIPTION	POST. REF.	ACCOUNTS RECEIVABLE CREDIT	SALES TAX PAYABLE CREDIT	SALES CREDIT	OTHER ACCOUNTS CREDIT			CASH DEBIT
						ACCOUNT NAME	POST. REF.	AMOUNT	

EXERCISE 9.2

CASH PAYMENTS JOURNAL

PAGE____

DATE	CK. NO.	DESCRIPTION	POST. REF.	ACCOUNTS PAYABLE DEBIT	OTHER ACCOUNTS DEBIT			PURCHASES DISCOUNT CREDIT	CASH CREDIT
					ACCOUNT NAME	POST. REF.	AMOUNT		

Copyright © 2017 by McGraw-Hill Education. All rights reserved.

Name

EXERCISES 9.3, 9.4

EXERCISE 9.3

CASH PAYMENTS JOURNAL

PAGE

DATE	CK. NO.	DESCRIPTION	POST. REF.	ACCOUNTS PAYABLE DEBIT	OTHER ACCOUNTS DEBIT			PURCHASES DISCOUNT CREDIT	CASH CREDIT
					ACCOUNT NAME	POST. REF.	AMOUNT		

EXERCISE 9.4

CASH PAYMENTS JOURNAL

PAGE

DATE	CK. NO.	DESCRIPTION	POST. REF.	ACCOUNTS PAYABLE DEBIT	OTHER ACCOUNTS DEBIT			PURCHASES DISCOUNT CREDIT	CASH CREDIT
					ACCOUNT NAME	POST. REF.	AMOUNT		

Copyright © 2017 by McGraw-Hill Education. All rights reserved.

Name

EXERCISE 9.5

GENERAL JOURNAL PAGE______

	DATE		DESCRIPTION	POST. REF.	DEBIT	CREDIT	
1							1
2							2
3							3
4							4
5							5
6							6
7							7
8							8
9							9
10							10
11							11
12							12
13							13
14							14

Copyright © 2017 by McGraw-Hill Education. All rights reserved.

Name ______________________

EXERCISE 9.6

	Bank Balance	Book Balance	Accounting Entry
1.			
2.			
3.			
4.			
5.			
6.			
7.			

EXTRA FORM

GENERAL JOURNAL PAGE________

	DATE		DESCRIPTION	POST. REF.	DEBIT	CREDIT	
1							1
2							2
3							3
4							4
5							5
6							6
7							7
8							8
9							9
10							10
11							11
12							12
13							13
14							14

Copyright © 2017 by McGraw-Hill Education. All rights reserved.

Name

EXERCISE 9.7

Copyright © 2017 by McGraw-Hill Education. All rights reserved.

Name ______________________________

EXERCISE 9.7 (continued)

GENERAL JOURNAL PAGE________

	DATE		DESCRIPTION	POST. REF.	DEBIT	CREDIT	
1							1
2							2
3							3
4							4
5							5
6							6
7							7
8							8
9							9
10							10
11							11
12							12

Copyright © 2017 by McGraw-Hill Education. All rights reserved.

Name

EXERCISE 9.8

Copyright © 2017 by McGraw-Hill Education. All rights reserved.

Name

EXERCISE 9.9

GENERAL JOURNAL PAGE 21

	DATE		DESCRIPTION	POST. REF.	DEBIT	CREDIT	
1							1
2							2
3							3
4							4
5							5
6							6
7							7
8							8
9							9
10							10
11							11
12							12
13							13
14							14

EXERCISE 9.10 APP

Merchandise Inventory ________

Sales Tax Payable ________

Sales ________

Sales Discounts ________

Sales Returns and Allowances ________

Cost of Goods Sold ________

Credit Card Expense ________

Copyright © 2017 by McGraw-Hill Education. All rights reserved.

Name ____________________

EXERCISE 9.11 APP

GENERAL JOURNAL PAGE________

DATE		DESCRIPTION	POST. REF.	DEBIT	CREDIT

EXERCISE 9.12 APP

GENERAL JOURNAL PAGE________

DATE		DESCRIPTION	POST. REF.	DEBIT	CREDIT

Copyright © 2017 by McGraw-Hill Education. All rights reserved.

Name

EXERCISE 9.12 APP (continued)

GENERAL JOURNAL PAGE

	DATE		DESCRIPTION	POST. REF.	DEBIT	CREDIT	
18							18
19							19
20							20
21							21
22							22
23							23
24							24
25							25
26							26
27							27

EXERCISE 9.13 APP

GENERAL JOURNAL PAGE 1

	DATE		DESCRIPTION	POST. REF.	DEBIT	CREDIT	
1							1
2							2
3							3
4							4
5							5
6							6
7							7
8							8
9							9
10							10
11							11
12							12
13							13
14							14
15							15
16							16
17							17
18							18

 Copyright © 2017 by McGraw-Hill Education. All rights reserved.

Name ____________________

EXERCISE 9.14 APP

GENERAL JOURNAL PAGE 1

	DATE		DESCRIPTION	POST. REF.	DEBIT	CREDIT	
1							1
2							2
3							3
4							4
5							5
6							6
7							7
8							8
9							9
10							10
11							11
12							12
13							13
14							14
15							15
16							16
17							17
18							18
19							19
20							20
21							21
22							22
23							23
24							24
25							25
26							26
27							27
28							28
29							29
30							30
31							31
32							32
33							33
34							34
35							35
36							36
37							37

Copyright © 2017 by McGraw-Hill Education. All rights reserved.

Name ______________________

EXERCISE 9.15 APP

GENERAL JOURNAL — PAGE 1

	DATE		DESCRIPTION	POST. REF.	DEBIT	CREDIT	
1							1
2							2
3							3
4							4
5							5
6							6
7							7
8							8
9							9
10							10
11							11
12							12
13							13

EXERCISE 9.16 APP

Bushard Company: ______________________

GENERAL JOURNAL — PAGE 20

	DATE		DESCRIPTION	POST. REF.	DEBIT	CREDIT	
1							1
2							2
3							3
4							4
5							5
6							6
7							7
8							8
9							9
10							10
11							11
12							12
13							13
14							14
15							15
16							16
17							17

Copyright © 2017 by McGraw-Hill Education. All rights reserved.

Name ______________________________

EXERCISE 9.16 APP (continued)

Schmidt, Inc.: ______________________________

GENERAL JOURNAL PAGE 20

DATE		DESCRIPTION	POST. REF.	DEBIT	CREDIT

Copyright © 2017 by McGraw-Hill Education. All rights reserved.

Name ____________________

PROBLEM 9.1A or 9.1B

CASH RECEIPTS JOURNAL

PAGE ____

DATE	DESCRIPTION	POST. REF.	ACCOUNTS RECEIVABLE CREDIT	SALES TAX PAYABLE CREDIT	SALES CREDIT	OTHER ACCOUNTS CREDIT			CASH DEBIT
						ACCOUNT NAME	POST. REF.	AMOUNT	

Copyright © 2017 by McGraw-Hill Education. All rights reserved.

Name ______________________________

PROBLEM 9.1A or 9.1B (continued)

GENERAL LEDGER

ACCOUNT ______________________________ ACCOUNT NO. ________

DATE		DESCRIPTION	POST. REF.	DEBIT	CREDIT	BALANCE DEBIT	BALANCE CREDIT

ACCOUNT ______________________________ ACCOUNT NO. ________

DATE		DESCRIPTION	POST. REF.	DEBIT	CREDIT	BALANCE DEBIT	BALANCE CREDIT

ACCOUNT ______________________________ ACCOUNT NO. ________

DATE		DESCRIPTION	POST. REF.	DEBIT	CREDIT	BALANCE DEBIT	BALANCE CREDIT

ACCOUNT ______________________________ ACCOUNT NO. ________

DATE		DESCRIPTION	POST. REF.	DEBIT	CREDIT	BALANCE DEBIT	BALANCE CREDIT

ACCOUNT ______________________________ ACCOUNT NO. ________

DATE		DESCRIPTION	POST. REF.	DEBIT	CREDIT	BALANCE DEBIT	BALANCE CREDIT

Copyright © 2017 by McGraw-Hill Education. All rights reserved.

Name ______________________

PROBLEM 9.1A or 9.1B (continued)

GENERAL LEDGER

ACCOUNT ______________________ ACCOUNT NO. ________

DATE	DESCRIPTION	POST. REF.	DEBIT	CREDIT	BALANCE DEBIT	BALANCE CREDIT

ACCOUNT ______________________ ACCOUNT NO. ________

DATE	DESCRIPTION	POST. REF.	DEBIT	CREDIT	BALANCE DEBIT	BALANCE CREDIT

ACCOUNT ______________________ ACCOUNT NO. ________

DATE	DESCRIPTION	POST. REF.	DEBIT	CREDIT	BALANCE DEBIT	BALANCE CREDIT

ACCOUNT ______________________ ACCOUNT NO. ________

DATE	DESCRIPTION	POST. REF.	DEBIT	CREDIT	BALANCE DEBIT	BALANCE CREDIT

Analyze: ______________________

Copyright © 2017 by McGraw-Hill Education. All rights reserved.

Name ______________________________

PROBLEM 9.2A or 9.2B

CASH PAYMENTS JOURNAL

PAGE______

DATE	CK. NO.	DESCRIPTION	POST. REF.	ACCOUNTS PAYABLE DEBIT	OTHER ACCOUNTS DEBIT			PURCHASES DISCOUNT CREDIT	CASH CREDIT
					ACCOUNT NAME	POST. REF.	AMOUNT		

Copyright © 2017 by McGraw-Hill Education. All rights reserved.

Name ____________________

PROBLEM 9.2A or 9.2B (continued)

PETTY CASH ANALYSIS SHEET

PAGE____

DATE	VOU. NO.	DESCRIPTION	RECEIPTS	PAYMENTS	DISTRIBUTION OF PAYMENTS				
					SUPPLIES DEBIT	DELIVERY EXPENSE DEBIT	MISC. EXPENSE DEBIT	OTHER ACCOUNTS DEBIT	
								ACCOUNT NAME	AMOUNT

Copyright © 2017 by McGraw-Hill Education. All rights reserved.

Name ______________________________

PROBLEM 9.2A or 9.2B (continued)

GENERAL LEDGER

ACCOUNT ______________________________ ACCOUNT NO. ________

DATE	DESCRIPTION	POST. REF.	DEBIT	CREDIT	BALANCE DEBIT	BALANCE CREDIT

ACCOUNT ______________________________ ACCOUNT NO. ________

DATE	DESCRIPTION	POST. REF.	DEBIT	CREDIT	BALANCE DEBIT	BALANCE CREDIT

ACCOUNT ______________________________ ACCOUNT NO. ________

DATE	DESCRIPTION	POST. REF.	DEBIT	CREDIT	BALANCE DEBIT	BALANCE CREDIT

ACCOUNT ______________________________ ACCOUNT NO. ________

DATE	DESCRIPTION	POST. REF.	DEBIT	CREDIT	BALANCE DEBIT	BALANCE CREDIT

ACCOUNT ______________________________ ACCOUNT NO. ________

DATE	DESCRIPTION	POST. REF.	DEBIT	CREDIT	BALANCE DEBIT	BALANCE CREDIT

Copyright © 2017 by McGraw-Hill Education. All rights reserved.

Name

PROBLEM 9.2A or 9.2B (continued)

GENERAL LEDGER

ACCOUNT ______________________ ACCOUNT NO. ________

DATE	DESCRIPTION	POST. REF.	DEBIT	CREDIT	BALANCE	
					DEBIT	CREDIT

ACCOUNT ______________________ ACCOUNT NO. ________

DATE	DESCRIPTION	POST. REF.	DEBIT	CREDIT	BALANCE	
					DEBIT	CREDIT

ACCOUNT ______________________ ACCOUNT NO. ________

DATE	DESCRIPTION	POST. REF.	DEBIT	CREDIT	BALANCE	
					DEBIT	CREDIT

ACCOUNT ______________________ ACCOUNT NO. ________

DATE	DESCRIPTION	POST. REF.	DEBIT	CREDIT	BALANCE	
					DEBIT	CREDIT

ACCOUNT ______________________ ACCOUNT NO. ________

DATE	DESCRIPTION	POST. REF.	DEBIT	CREDIT	BALANCE	
					DEBIT	CREDIT

Analyze: ______________________

Copyright © 2017 by McGraw-Hill Education. All rights reserved.

Name ____________________

PROBLEM 9.2A or 9.2B (continued)

GENERAL LEDGER

ACCOUNT ____________________ ACCOUNT NO. ________

DATE		DESCRIPTION	POST. REF.	DEBIT	CREDIT	BALANCE DEBIT	BALANCE CREDIT

ACCOUNT ____________________ ACCOUNT NO. ________

DATE		DESCRIPTION	POST. REF.	DEBIT	CREDIT	BALANCE DEBIT	BALANCE CREDIT

ACCOUNT ____________________ ACCOUNT NO. ________

DATE		DESCRIPTION	POST. REF.	DEBIT	CREDIT	BALANCE DEBIT	BALANCE CREDIT

ACCOUNT ____________________ ACCOUNT NO. ________

DATE		DESCRIPTION	POST. REF.	DEBIT	CREDIT	BALANCE DEBIT	BALANCE CREDIT

ACCOUNT ____________________ ACCOUNT NO. ________

DATE		DESCRIPTION	POST. REF.	DEBIT	CREDIT	BALANCE DEBIT	BALANCE CREDIT

Analyze: ____________________

Copyright © 2017 by McGraw-Hill Education. All rights reserved.

Name ______________________________

PROBLEM 9.3A or 9.3B

SALES JOURNAL

PAGE ______

	DATE	INVOICE NO.	CUSTOMER'S NAME	POST. REF.	ACCOUNTS RECEIVABLE DR./ SALES CR.	
1						1
2						2
3						3
4						4
5						5
6						6
7						7
8						8
9						9
10						10
11						11

CASH RECEIPTS JOURNAL

PAGE ______

DATE	DESCRIPTION	POST. REF.	ACCOUNTS RECEIVABLE CREDIT	SALES CREDIT	OTHER ACCOUNTS CREDIT			SALES DISCOUNTS DEBIT	CASH DEBIT
					ACCOUNT NAME	POST. REF.	AMOUNT		

Copyright © 2017 by McGraw-Hill Education. All rights reserved.

Name ______________________

PROBLEM 9.3A or 9.3B (continued)

GENERAL JOURNAL PAGE______

	DATE		DESCRIPTION	POST. REF.	DEBIT	CREDIT	
1							1
2							2
3							3
4							4
5							5
6							6
7							7
8							8
9							9
10							10
11							11
12							12

GENERAL LEDGER (PARTIAL)

ACCOUNT ______________________ ACCOUNT NO. ________

DATE		DESCRIPTION	POST. REF.	DEBIT	CREDIT	BALANCE	
						DEBIT	CREDIT

ACCOUNT ______________________ ACCOUNT NO. ________

DATE		DESCRIPTION	POST. REF.	DEBIT	CREDIT	BALANCE	
						DEBIT	CREDIT

ACCOUNT ______________________ ACCOUNT NO. ________

DATE		DESCRIPTION	POST. REF.	DEBIT	CREDIT	BALANCE	
						DEBIT	CREDIT

Copyright © 2017 by McGraw-Hill Education. All rights reserved.

Name ______________________

PROBLEM 9.3A or 9.3B (continued)

GENERAL LEDGER (PARTIAL)

ACCOUNT ______________________ ACCOUNT NO. ________

DATE		DESCRIPTION	POST. REF.	DEBIT	CREDIT	BALANCE	
						DEBIT	CREDIT

ACCOUNT ______________________ ACCOUNT NO. ________

DATE		DESCRIPTION	POST. REF.	DEBIT	CREDIT	BALANCE	
						DEBIT	CREDIT

ACCOUNT ______________________ ACCOUNT NO. ________

DATE		DESCRIPTION	POST. REF.	DEBIT	CREDIT	BALANCE	
						DEBIT	CREDIT

Analyze: ______________________

Copyright © 2017 by McGraw-Hill Education. All rights reserved.

Name

PROBLEM 9.4A or 9.4B

PURCHASES JOURNAL PAGE

DATE		PURCHASED FROM	INVOICE NUMBER	INVOICE DATE	TERMS	POST. REF.	PURCHASES DR./ ACCOUNTS PAYABLE CR.

GENERAL JOURNAL PAGE

	DATE		DESCRIPTION	POST. REF.	DEBIT	CREDIT	
1							1
2							2
3							3
4							4
5							5
6							6
7							7
8							8
9							9
10							10
11							11
12							12
13							13
14							14
15							15
16							16
17							17
18							18
19							19
20							20
21							21
22							22
23							23

Copyright © 2017 by McGraw-Hill Education. All rights reserved.

Name ______________________

PROBLEM 9.4A or 9.4B (continued)

CASH PAYMENTS JOURNAL

PAGE ______

DATE	CK. NO.	DESCRIPTION	POST. REF.	ACCOUNTS PAYABLE DEBIT	OTHER ACCOUNTS DEBIT ACCOUNT NAME	OTHER ACCOUNTS DEBIT POST. REF.	OTHER ACCOUNTS DEBIT AMOUNT	PURCHASES DISCOUNT CREDIT	CASH CREDIT

Copyright © 2017 by McGraw-Hill Education. All rights reserved.

Name ____________________

PROBLEM 9.4A or 9.4B (continued)

GENERAL LEDGER

ACCOUNT ____________________ ACCOUNT NO. ________

DATE		DESCRIPTION	POST. REF.	DEBIT	CREDIT	BALANCE	
						DEBIT	CREDIT

ACCOUNT ____________________ ACCOUNT NO. ________

DATE		DESCRIPTION	POST. REF.	DEBIT	CREDIT	BALANCE	
						DEBIT	CREDIT

ACCOUNT ____________________ ACCOUNT NO. ________

DATE		DESCRIPTION	POST. REF.	DEBIT	CREDIT	BALANCE	
						DEBIT	CREDIT

ACCOUNT ____________________ ACCOUNT NO. ________

DATE		DESCRIPTION	POST. REF.	DEBIT	CREDIT	BALANCE	
						DEBIT	CREDIT

Copyright © 2017 by McGraw-Hill Education. All rights reserved.

Name ____________________

PROBLEM 9.4A or 9.4B (continued)

GENERAL LEDGER

ACCOUNT ____________________ ACCOUNT NO. __________

DATE		DESCRIPTION	POST. REF.	DEBIT	CREDIT	BALANCE	
						DEBIT	CREDIT

ACCOUNT ____________________ ACCOUNT NO. __________

DATE		DESCRIPTION	POST. REF.	DEBIT	CREDIT	BALANCE	
						DEBIT	CREDIT

ACCOUNT ____________________ ACCOUNT NO. __________

DATE		DESCRIPTION	POST. REF.	DEBIT	CREDIT	BALANCE	
						DEBIT	CREDIT

ACCOUNT ____________________ ACCOUNT NO. __________

DATE		DESCRIPTION	POST. REF.	DEBIT	CREDIT	BALANCE	
						DEBIT	CREDIT

ACCOUNT ____________________ ACCOUNT NO. __________

DATE		DESCRIPTION	POST. REF.	DEBIT	CREDIT	BALANCE	
						DEBIT	CREDIT

ACCOUNT ____________________ ACCOUNT NO. __________

DATE		DESCRIPTION	POST. REF.	DEBIT	CREDIT	BALANCE	
						DEBIT	CREDIT

Copyright © 2017 by McGraw-Hill Education. All rights reserved.

Name

PROBLEM 9.4A or 9.4B (continued)

Analyze:

EXTRA FORM

Name

PROBLEM 9.5A or 9.5B

GENERAL JOURNAL

PAGE

	DATE		DESCRIPTION	POST. REF.	DEBIT	CREDIT	
1							1
2							2
3							3
4							4
5							5
6							6
7							7
8							8
9							9
10							10
11							11
12							12
13							13

Analyze:

Copyright © 2017 by McGraw-Hill Education. All rights reserved.

Name

PROBLEM 9.6A or 9.6B

Copyright © 2017 by McGraw-Hill Education. All rights reserved.

Name ______________________

PROBLEM 9.6A or 9.6B (continued)

GENERAL JOURNAL PAGE______

	DATE		DESCRIPTION	POST. REF.	DEBIT	CREDIT	
1							1
2							2
3							3
4							4
5							5
6							6
7							7
8							8
9							9
10							10
11							11
12							12
13							13
14							14
15							15
16							16
17							17
18							18
19							19
20							20
21							21
22							22
23							23
24							24
25							25
26							26
27							27
28							28

Analyze: ______________________

Copyright © 2017 by McGraw-Hill Education. All rights reserved.

Name ____________________

PROBLEM 9.7A or 9.7B

GENERAL JOURNAL PAGE ______

	DATE		DESCRIPTION	POST. REF.	DEBIT	CREDIT	
1							1
2							2
3							3
4							4
5							5
6							6
7							7
8							8
9							9
10							10
11							11
12							12
13							13

Analyze: ____________________

Copyright © 2017 by McGraw-Hill Education. All rights reserved.

Name

PROBLEM 9.8A or 9.8B

Copyright © 2017 by McGraw-Hill Education. All rights reserved.

Name ____________________

PROBLEM 9.8A or 9.8B (continued)

GENERAL JOURNAL

PAGE ________

	DATE		DESCRIPTION	POST. REF.	DEBIT	CREDIT	
1							1
2							2
3							3
4							4
5							5
6							6
7							7
8							8
9							9
10							10
11							11
12							12
13							13
14							14
15							15
16							16
17							17
18							18
19							19
20							20
21							21
22							22
23							23
24							24
25							25
26							26
27							27
28							28

Analyze: ____________________

Copyright © 2017 by McGraw-Hill Education. All rights reserved.

Name

PROBLEM 9.9A or 9.9B APP

GENERAL JOURNAL PAGE______

DATE		DESCRIPTION	POST. REF.	DEBIT	CREDIT

Copyright © 2017 by McGraw-Hill Education. All rights reserved.

Name ______________________

PROBLEM 9.9A or 9.9B APP (continued)

GENERAL JOURNAL PAGE ________

DATE	DESCRIPTION	POST. REF.	DEBIT	CREDIT

Analyze: ______________________

Copyright © 2017 by McGraw-Hill Education. All rights reserved.

Name ____________________

CRITICAL THINKING PROBLEM 9.1

SALES JOURNAL

PAGE ________

	DATE	SALES SLIP NO.	CUSTOMER'S NAME	POST. REF.	ACCOUNTS RECEIVABLE DEBIT	SALES TAX PAYABLE CREDIT	SALES CREDIT	
1								1
2								2
3								3
4								4
5								5
6								6
7								7
8								8
9								9
10								10
11								11
12								12
13								13
14								14
15								15
16								16

PURCHASES JOURNAL

PAGE ________

DATE	PURCHASED FROM	INVOICE NUMBER	INVOICE DATE	TERMS	POST. REF.	ACCOUNTS PAYABLE CREDIT	PURCHASES DEBIT	FREIGHT IN DEBIT

Copyright © 2017 by McGraw-Hill Education. All rights reserved.

Name

CRITICAL THINKING PROBLEM 9.1 (continued)

GENERAL JOURNAL

PAGE________

DATE	DESCRIPTION	POST. REF.	DEBIT	CREDIT

Copyright © 2017 by McGraw-Hill Education. All rights reserved.

Name ____________________

CRITICAL THINKING PROBLEM 9.1 (continued)

CASH RECEIPTS JOURNAL

PAGE____

DATE	DESCRIPTION	POST. REF.	ACCOUNTS RECEIVABLE CREDIT	SALES TAX PAYABLE CREDIT	SALES CREDIT	OTHER ACCOUNTS CREDIT			CASH DEBIT
						ACCOUNT NAME	POST. REF.	AMOUNT	

Copyright © 2017 by McGraw-Hill Education. All rights reserved.

Name ____________________

CRITICAL THINKING PROBLEM 9.1 (continued)

CASH PAYMENTS JOURNAL

PAGE____

DATE	CK. NO.	DESCRIPTION	POST. REF.	ACCOUNTS PAYABLE DEBIT	OTHER ACCOUNTS DEBIT			PURCHASES DISCOUNT CREDIT	CASH CREDIT
					ACCOUNT NAME	POST. REF.	AMOUNT		

Copyright © 2017 by McGraw-Hill Education. All rights reserved.

Name ______________________

CRITICAL THINKING PROBLEM 9.1 (continued)

GENERAL LEDGER

ACCOUNT ______________________ ACCOUNT NO. ________

DATE		DESCRIPTION	POST. REF.	DEBIT	CREDIT	BALANCE DEBIT	BALANCE CREDIT

ACCOUNT ______________________ ACCOUNT NO. ________

DATE		DESCRIPTION	POST. REF.	DEBIT	CREDIT	BALANCE DEBIT	BALANCE CREDIT

ACCOUNT ______________________ ACCOUNT NO. ________

DATE		DESCRIPTION	POST. REF.	DEBIT	CREDIT	BALANCE DEBIT	BALANCE CREDIT

ACCOUNT ______________________ ACCOUNT NO. ________

DATE		DESCRIPTION	POST. REF.	DEBIT	CREDIT	BALANCE DEBIT	BALANCE CREDIT

ACCOUNT ______________________ ACCOUNT NO. ________

DATE		DESCRIPTION	POST. REF.	DEBIT	CREDIT	BALANCE DEBIT	BALANCE CREDIT

ACCOUNT ______________________ ACCOUNT NO. ________

DATE		DESCRIPTION	POST. REF.	DEBIT	CREDIT	BALANCE DEBIT	BALANCE CREDIT

Copyright © 2017 by McGraw-Hill Education. All rights reserved.

Name ______________________________

CRITICAL THINKING PROBLEM 9.1 (continued)

GENERAL LEDGER

ACCOUNT ______________________________ ACCOUNT NO. __________

DATE	DESCRIPTION	POST. REF.	DEBIT	CREDIT	BALANCE DEBIT	BALANCE CREDIT

ACCOUNT ______________________________ ACCOUNT NO. __________

DATE	DESCRIPTION	POST. REF.	DEBIT	CREDIT	BALANCE DEBIT	BALANCE CREDIT

ACCOUNT ______________________________ ACCOUNT NO. __________

DATE	DESCRIPTION	POST. REF.	DEBIT	CREDIT	BALANCE DEBIT	BALANCE CREDIT

ACCOUNT ______________________________ ACCOUNT NO. __________

DATE	DESCRIPTION	POST. REF.	DEBIT	CREDIT	BALANCE DEBIT	BALANCE CREDIT

ACCOUNT ______________________________ ACCOUNT NO. __________

DATE	DESCRIPTION	POST. REF.	DEBIT	CREDIT	BALANCE DEBIT	BALANCE CREDIT

Copyright © 2017 by McGraw-Hill Education. All rights reserved.

Name ______________________

CRITICAL THINKING PROBLEM 9.1 (continued)

GENERAL LEDGER

ACCOUNT ______________________ ACCOUNT NO. ________

DATE		DESCRIPTION	POST. REF.	DEBIT	CREDIT	BALANCE	
						DEBIT	CREDIT

ACCOUNT ______________________ ACCOUNT NO. ________

DATE		DESCRIPTION	POST. REF.	DEBIT	CREDIT	BALANCE	
						DEBIT	CREDIT

ACCOUNT ______________________ ACCOUNT NO. ________

DATE		DESCRIPTION	POST. REF.	DEBIT	CREDIT	BALANCE	
						DEBIT	CREDIT

ACCOUNT ______________________ ACCOUNT NO. ________

DATE		DESCRIPTION	POST. REF.	DEBIT	CREDIT	BALANCE	
						DEBIT	CREDIT

ACCOUNT ______________________ ACCOUNT NO. ________

DATE		DESCRIPTION	POST. REF.	DEBIT	CREDIT	BALANCE	
						DEBIT	CREDIT

Copyright © 2017 by McGraw-Hill Education. All rights reserved.

Name

CRITICAL THINKING PROBLEM 9.1 (continued)

GENERAL LEDGER

ACCOUNT ______ ACCOUNT NO. ______

DATE	DESCRIPTION	POST. REF.	DEBIT	CREDIT	BALANCE	
					DEBIT	CREDIT

ACCOUNT ______ ACCOUNT NO. ______

DATE	DESCRIPTION	POST. REF.	DEBIT	CREDIT	BALANCE	
					DEBIT	CREDIT

ACCOUNT ______ ACCOUNT NO. ______

DATE	DESCRIPTION	POST. REF.	DEBIT	CREDIT	BALANCE	
					DEBIT	CREDIT

ACCOUNTS RECEIVABLE SUBSIDIARY LEDGER

NAME ______ TERMS ______

DATE	DESCRIPTION	POST. REF.	DEBIT	CREDIT	BALANCE

NAME ______ TERMS ______

DATE	DESCRIPTION	POST. REF.	DEBIT	CREDIT	BALANCE

Copyright © 2017 by McGraw-Hill Education. All rights reserved.

Name

CRITICAL THINKING PROBLEM 9.1 (continued)

ACCOUNTS RECEIVABLE SUBSIDIARY LEDGER

NAME ______ TERMS ______

DATE		DESCRIPTION	POST. REF.	DEBIT	CREDIT	BALANCE

NAME ______ TERMS ______

DATE		DESCRIPTION	POST. REF.	DEBIT	CREDIT	BALANCE

NAME ______ TERMS ______

DATE		DESCRIPTION	POST. REF.	DEBIT	CREDIT	BALANCE

NAME ______ TERMS ______

DATE		DESCRIPTION	POST. REF.	DEBIT	CREDIT	BALANCE

NAME ______ TERMS ______

DATE		DESCRIPTION	POST. REF.	DEBIT	CREDIT	BALANCE

Copyright © 2017 by McGraw-Hill Education. All rights reserved.

Name

CRITICAL THINKING PROBLEM 9.1 (continued)

ACCOUNTS PAYABLE SUBSIDIARY LEDGER

NAME ____ TERMS ____

DATE		DESCRIPTION	POST. REF.	DEBIT	CREDIT	BALANCE

NAME ____ TERMS ____

DATE		DESCRIPTION	POST. REF.	DEBIT	CREDIT	BALANCE

NAME ____ TERMS ____

DATE		DESCRIPTION	POST. REF.	DEBIT	CREDIT	BALANCE

NAME ____ TERMS ____

DATE		DESCRIPTION	POST. REF.	DEBIT	CREDIT	BALANCE

Copyright © 2017 by McGraw-Hill Education. All rights reserved.

Name

CRITICAL THINKING PROBLEM 9.1 (continued)

NAME ______ TERMS ______

DATE		DESCRIPTION	POST. REF.	DEBIT	CREDIT	BALANCE

NAME ______ TERMS ______

DATE		DESCRIPTION	POST. REF.	DEBIT	CREDIT	BALANCE

ACCOUNTS PAYABLE SUBSIDIARY LEDGER

NAME ______ TERMS ______

DATE		DESCRIPTION	POST. REF.	DEBIT	CREDIT	BALANCE

Analyze: ______

Copyright © 2017 by McGraw-Hill Education. All rights reserved.

Name

CRITICAL THINKING PROBLEM 9.2

Copyright © 2017 by McGraw-Hill Education. All rights reserved.

Name

CRITICAL THINKING PROBLEM 9.2 (continued)

Copyright © 2017 by McGraw-Hill Education. All rights reserved.

WORKING PAPERS

Name ______________________________

EXERCISE 10.1

EMPLOYEE NO.	HOURLY RATE	HOURS WORKED	GROSS EARNINGS

EXERCISE 10.2

HOURLY RATE	OVERTIME RATE	REGULAR HOURS WORKED	OVERTIME HOURS WORKED	REGULAR PAY	OVERTIME PAY	GROSS PAY

EXERCISE 10.3

EMPLOYEE NO.	DECEMBER SALARY	YEAR TO DATE EARNINGS THROUGH NOVEMBER 30	SOC. SEC. TAXABLE EARNINGS-DECEMBER	SOCIAL SECURITY TAX 6.20%

EXERCISE 10.4

EMPLOYEE NO.	DECEMBER SALARY	MEDICARE TAXABLE EARNINGS-DECEMBER	MEDICARE TAX 1.45%

EXERCISE 10.5

EMPLOYEE NO.	MARITAL STATUS	WITHHOLDING ALLOWANCES	WEEKLY SALARY	INCOME TAX WITHHOLDING

Copyright © 2017 by McGraw-Hill Education. All rights reserved.

Name ____________________

EXERCISE 10.6

GENERAL JOURNAL — PAGE ______

	DATE		DESCRIPTION	POST. REF.	DEBIT	CREDIT	
1							1
2							2
3							3
4							4
5							5
6							6
7							7
8							8
9							9
10							10
11							11
12							12
13							13
14							14
15							15

EXERCISE 10.7

GENERAL JOURNAL — PAGE ______

	DATE		DESCRIPTION	POST. REF.	DEBIT	CREDIT	
1							1
2							2
3							3
4							4
5							5
6							6
7							7
8							8
9							9
10							10
11							11
12							12
13							13
14							14
15							15

Copyright © 2017 by McGraw-Hill Education. All rights reserved.

Name ______________________

PROBLEM 10.1A or 10.1B

EMPLOYEE NO.	REGULAR HOURS, HOURLY RATE	HOURS WORKED	REGULAR TIME EARNINGS	OVERTIME EARNINGS	GROSS EARNINGS

Gross Pay	
Social Security Tax	
Medicare Tax	
Income Tax Withholding	
Health & Disability	
Charitable Contribution	
Savings	
Net Pay	

GENERAL JOURNAL

PAGE______

	DATE		DESCRIPTION	POST. REF.	DEBIT	CREDIT	
1							1
2							2
3							3
4							4
5							5

Analyze: ______________________

Copyright © 2017 by McGraw-Hill Education. All rights reserved.

Name ______________________________

PROBLEM 10.2A or 10.2B

PAYROLL REGISTER WEEK BEGINNING ____________ AND ENDING ____________ PAID ____________

NAME	NO. OF ALLOW.	MARITAL STATUS	CUMULATIVE EARNINGS	NO. OF HRS.	RATE	EARNINGS			CUMULATIVE EARNINGS
						REGULAR TIME EARNINGS	OVERTIME EARNINGS	GROSS AMOUNT	

TAXABLE WAGES			DEDUCTIONS			DISTRIBUTION		
SOCIAL SECURITY	MEDICARE	FUTA	SOCIAL SECURITY	MEDICARE	INCOME TAX	NET AMOUNT	CHECK NO.	WAGES EXPENSE

Copyright © 2017 by McGraw-Hill Education. All rights reserved.

Name

PROBLEM 10.2A or 10.2B (continued)

Analyze:

GENERAL JOURNAL PAGE

DATE		DESCRIPTION	POST. REF.	DEBIT	CREDIT

Copyright © 2017 by McGraw-Hill Education. All rights reserved.

Name ____________________

PROBLEM 10.3A or 10.3B

PAYROLL REGISTER WEEK BEGINNING ____________ AND ENDING ____________ PAID ____________

NAME	NO. OF ALLOW.	MARITAL STATUS	CUMULATIVE EARNINGS	NO. OF HRS.	RATE	EARNINGS			CUMULATIVE EARNINGS	TAXABLE WAGES			DEDUCTIONS			NET AMOUNT	CHECK NO.	DISTRIBUTION	
						REGULAR TIME EARNINGS	OVERTIME EARNINGS	GROSS AMOUNT		SOCIAL SECURITY	MEDICARE	FUTA	SOCIAL SECURITY	MEDICARE	INCOME TAX			OFFICE WAGES	DELIVERY WAGES

Copyright © 2017 by McGraw-Hill Education. All rights reserved.

PROBLEM 10.3A or 10.3B (continued)

Analyze:

GENERAL JOURNAL PAGE

DATE	DESCRIPTION	POST. REF.	DEBIT	CREDIT

Copyright © 2017 by McGraw-Hill Education. All rights reserved.

Name

PROBLEM 10.4A or 10.4B

EMPLOYEE NAME	CUMULATIVE EARNINGS	MONTHLY PAY	SOCIAL SECURITY	MEDICARE	EMPLOYEE INCOME TAX WITHHOLDING	NET PAY
Totals						

GENERAL JOURNAL PAGE

	DATE		DESCRIPTION	POST. REF.	DEBIT	CREDIT	
1							1
2							2
3							3
4							4
5							5
6							6
7							7
8							8
9							9
10							10
11							11
12							12
13							13
14							14
15							15
16							16
17							17
18							18
19							19
20							20
21							21
22							22
23							23
24							24
25							25
26							26

Analyze:

Copyright © 2017 by McGraw-Hill Education. All rights reserved.

Name ______________________

CRITICAL THINKING PROBLEM 10.1

EMPLOYEE NAME	CUMULATIVE EARNINGS	MONTHLY PAY	SOCIAL SECURITY	MEDICARE	EMPLOYEE INCOME TAX WITHHOLDING	NET PAY

GENERAL JOURNAL PAGE ______

	DATE		DESCRIPTION	POST. REF.	DEBIT	CREDIT	
1							1
2							2
3							3
4							4
5							5
6							6
7							7
8							8
9							9
10							10
11							11
12							12
13							13
14							14
15							15

Analyze: ______________________

Copyright © 2017 by McGraw-Hill Education. All rights reserved.

Name

CRITICAL THINKING PROBLEM 10.2

Copyright © 2017 by McGraw-Hill Education. All rights reserved.

WORKING PAPERS

Name ______________________________

EXERCISE 11.1

____

____

____

____

____

EXERCISE 11.2

GENERAL JOURNAL — PAGE______

	DATE		DESCRIPTION	POST. REF.	DEBIT	CREDIT	
1							1
2							2
3							3
4							4
5							5
6							6
7							7

EXERCISE 11.3

TAX	BASE	RATE	AMOUNT

EXERCISE 11.4

GENERAL JOURNAL — PAGE______

	DATE		DESCRIPTION	POST. REF.	DEBIT	CREDIT	
1							1
2							2
3							3
4							4
5							5
6							6
7							7

Copyright © 2017 by McGraw-Hill Education. All rights reserved.

Name ________________

EXERCISE 11.5

EXERCISE 11.6

GENERAL JOURNAL

PAGE ________

	DATE		DESCRIPTION	POST. REF.	DEBIT	CREDIT	
1							1
2							2
3							3
4							4
5							5
6							6
7							7

EXERCISE 11.7

EXERCISE 11.8

WORK CLASSIFICATION	ESTIMATED EARNINGS	RATE	ESTIMATED PREMIUM

Copyright © 2017 by McGraw-Hill Education. All rights reserved.

Name

PROBLEM 11.1A or 11.1B

TAX	BASE	RATE	AMOUNT

GENERAL JOURNAL PAGE 28

	DATE		DESCRIPTION	POST. REF.	DEBIT	CREDIT	
1							1
2							2
3							3
4							4
5							5
6							6
7							7
8							8
9							9
10							10
11							11
12							12

Analyze:

Copyright © 2017 by McGraw-Hill Education. All rights reserved.

Name

PROBLEM 11.2A or 11.2B

GENERAL JOURNAL

PAGE

DATE		DESCRIPTION	POST. REF.	DEBIT	CREDIT	
1						1
2						2
3						3
4						4
5						5
6						6
7						7
8						8
9						9
10						10
11						11
12						12
13						13
14						14
15						15
16						16
17						17
18						18
19						19
20						20
21						21
22						22
23						23
24						24
25						25
26						26
27						27
28						28
29						29
30						30
31						31
32						32
33						33

Analyze:

Copyright © 2017 by McGraw-Hill Education. All rights reserved.

Name ______________________

PROBLEM 11.3A or 11.3B

GENERAL JOURNAL

PAGE______

	DATE		DESCRIPTION	POST. REF.	DEBIT	CREDIT	
1							1
2							2
3							3
4							4
5							5
6							6
7							7
8							8
9							9
10							10
11							11
12							12
13							13
14							14
15							15
16							16
17							17
18							18
19							19
20							20
21							21
22							22
23							23
24							24
25							25
26							26
27							27
28							28
29							29
30							30
31							31
32							32
33							33

Analyze: ______________________

____

Copyright © 2017 by McGraw-Hill Education. All rights reserved.

Name ______________________________

PROBLEM 11.3A or 11.3B (continued)

Form **941 for 2019: Employer's Quarterly Federal Tax Return** 9901

(Rev. January 2005) Department of the Treasury — Internal Revenue Service OMB No. 1545-0029

Employer identification number ☐☐ – ☐☐☐☐☐☐☐

Name *(not your trade name)* ______________________

Trade name *(if any)* ______________________

Address ______________________

Number Street Suite or room number

____

City State ZIP code

Report for this Quarter ...
(Check one.)

☐ **1:** January, February, March

☒ **2:** April, May, June

☐ **3:** July, August, September

☐ **4:** October, November, December

Read the separate instructions before you fill out this form. Please type or print within the boxes.

Part 1: Answer these questions for this quarter.

1 **Number of employees who received wages, tips, or other compensation for the pay period including:** ***Mar. 12*** **(Quarter 1),** ***June 12*** **(Quarter 2),** ***Sept. 12*** **(Quarter 3),** ***Dec. 12*** **(Quarter 4)** 1 ______

2 **Wages, tips, and other compensation** . . . . 2 ______ .

3 **Total income tax withheld from wages, tips, and other compensation** . . . . 3 ______ .

4 **If no wages, tips, and other compensation are subject to social security or Medicare tax** . ☐ Check and go to line 6.

5 **Taxable social security and Medicare wages and tips:**

	Column 1		*Column 2*
5a **Taxable social security wages**	.	× .124 =	.
5b **Taxable social security tips**	.	× .124 =	.
5c **Taxable Medicare wages & tips**	.	× .029 =	.

5d **Total social security and Medicare taxes** (*Column 2,* lines 5a + 5b + 5c = line 5d) . 5d ______ .

6 **Total taxes before adjustments** (lines 3 + 5d = line 6) . . . . 6 ______ .

7 **Tax adjustments** (If your answer is a negative number, write it in brackets.):

7a **Current quarter's fractions of cents** . . . . ______ .

7b **Current quarter's sick pay** . . . . ______ .

7c **Current quarter's adjustments for tips and group-term life insurance** ______ .

7d **Current year's income tax withholding** (Attach Form 941c) . . ______ .

7e **Prior quarters' social security and Medicare taxes** (Attach Form 941c) ______ .

7f **Special additions to federal income tax** (reserved use) . . . . ______ .

7g **Special additions to social security and Medicare** (reserved use) ______ .

7h **Total adjustments** (Combine all amounts: lines 7a through 7g.) . . . . 7h ______ .

8 **Total taxes after adjustments** (Combine lines 6 and 7h.) . . . . 8 ______ .

9 **Advance earned income credit (EIC) payments made to employees** . . . . 9 ______ .

10 **Total taxes after adjustment for advance EIC** (lines 8 – 9 = line 10) . . . . 10 ______ .

11 **Total deposits for this quarter, including overpayment applied from a prior quarter** . . 11 ______ .

12 **Balance due** (lines 10 – 11 = line 12) Make checks payable to the *United States Treasury* . 12 ______ .

13 **Overpayment** (If line 11 is more than line 10, write the difference here.) ______ . Check one ☐ Apply to next return. ☐ Send a refund.

Next ➔

For Privacy Act and Paperwork Reduction Act Notice, see the back of the Payment Voucher. Cat. No. 17001Z Form **941**

Copyright © 2017 by McGraw-Hill Education. All rights reserved.

Name ______________________

PROBLEM 11.3A or 11.3B (continued)

9902

Name (not your trade name)	Employer identification number

Part 2: Tell us about your deposit schedule for this quarter.

If you are unsure about whether you are a monthly schedule depositor or a semiweekly schedule depositor, see *Pub. 15 (Circular E)*, section 11.

14 ☐☐ **Write the state abbreviation for the state where you made your deposits** OR **write "MU" if you made your deposits in *multiple* states.**

15 Check one: ☐ **Line 10 is less than $2,500.** Go to Part 3.

☐ **You were a monthly schedule depositor for the entire quarter. Fill out your tax liability for each month.** Then go to Part 3.

Tax liability: Month 1 ______ .

Month 2 ______ .

Month 3 ______ .

Total ______ . **Total must equal line 10.**

☐ **You were a semiweekly schedule depositor for any part of this quarter.** Fill out *Schedule B (Form 941): Report of Tax Liability for Semiweekly Schedule Depositors,* and attach it to this form.

Part 3: Tell us about your business. If a question does NOT apply to your business, leave it blank.

16 If your business has closed and you do not have to file returns in the future . . . . ☐ Check here, and

enter the final date you paid wages / / .

17 If you are a seasonal employer and you do not have to file a return for every quarter of the year . ☐ Check here.

Part 4: May we contact your third-party designee?

Do you want to allow an employee, a paid tax preparer, or another person to discuss this return with the IRS? See the instructions for details.

☐ Yes. Designee's name ______

Phone (   )   –   Personal Identification Number (PIN) ☐☐☐☐☐

☐ No.

Part 5: Sign here

Under penalties of perjury, I declare that I have examined this return, including accompanying schedules and statements, and to the best of my knowledge and belief, it is true, correct, and complete.

✗ Sign your name here ______

Print name and title ______

Date / /   Phone (   )   –

Part 6: For paid preparers only *(optional)*

Preparer's signature ______

Firm's name ______

Address ______   EIN ______

ZIP code ______

Date / /   Phone (   )   –   SSN/PTIN ______

☐ Check if you are self-employed.

Page **2**   Form **941**

Copyright © 2017 by McGraw-Hill Education. All rights reserved.

Name

PROBLEM 11.4A or 11.4B

GENERAL JOURNAL

PAGE

	DATE		DESCRIPTION	POST. REF.	DEBIT	CREDIT	
1							1
2							2
3							3
4							4
5							5
6							6
7							7
8							8
9							9
10							10
11							11
12							12
13							13
14							14
15							15
16							16
17							17
18							18
19							19
20							20
21							21
22							22
23							23
24							24
25							25
26							26
27							27
28							28
29							29

Analyze:

Copyright © 2017 by McGraw-Hill Education. All rights reserved.

Name

PROBLEM 11.5A or 11.5B

GENERAL JOURNAL PAGE

	DATE		DESCRIPTION	POST. REF.	DEBIT	CREDIT	
1							1
2							2
3							3
4							4
5							5
6							6
7							7
8							8
9							9
10							10
11							11
12							12
13							13
14							14
15							15
16							16
17							17
18							18
19							19
20							20
21							21
22							22
23							23
24							24
25							25
26							26
27							27
28							28
29							29
30							30
31							31
32							32
33							33
34							34

Analyze:

Copyright © 2017 by McGraw-Hill Education. All rights reserved.

Name ______________________

PROBLEM 11.5A or 11.5B (continued)

Form **940-EZ**

Department of the Treasury
Internal Revenue Service

Employer's Annual Federal Unemployment (FUTA) Tax Return

▶ See the separate Instructions for Form 940-EZ for information on completing this form.

OMB No. 1545-1110

2019

T	
FF	
FD	
FP	
I	
T	

You must complete this section. ▶

Name (as distinguished from trade name) | Calendar year

Trade name, if any | Employer identification number (EIN)

Address (number and street) | City, state, and ZIP code

Answer the questions under ***Who May Use Form 940-EZ*** *on page 2. If you cannot use Form 940-EZ, you must use Form 940.*

A Enter the amount of contributions paid to your state unemployment fund (see the separate instructions) . . ▶ $ ____________

B (1) Enter the name of the state where you have to pay contributions . . . . ▶ ____________

(2) Enter your state reporting number as shown on your state unemployment tax return ▶

If you will not have to file returns in the future, check here (see **Who Must File** in separate instructions) **and complete and sign the return.** ▶ ☐

If this is an Amended Return, check here (see **Amended Returns** in the separate instructions) . . . . ▶ ☐

Part I Taxable Wages and FUTA Tax

1	Total payments (including payments shown on lines 2 and 3) during the calendar year for services of employees			1	
2	Exempt payments. (Explain all exempt payments, attaching additional sheets if necessary.) ▶ ____________	2			
3	Payments of more than $7,000 for services. Enter only amounts over the first $7,000 paid to each employee **(see the separate instructions)**	3			
4	Add lines 2 and 3			4	
5	**Total taxable wages** (subtract line 4 from line 1) . . . . ▶			5	
6	**FUTA tax.** Multiply the wages on line 5 by .006 and enter here. **(If the result is over $100, also complete Part II.)**			6	
7	Total FUTA tax deposited for the year, including any overpayment applied from a prior year			7	
8	**Balance due** (subtract line 7 from line 6). Pay to the "United States Treasury." . . . . ▶ If you owe more than $100, see **Depositing FUTA tax** in the separate instructions.			8	
9	**Overpayment** (subtract line 6 from line 7). Check if it is to be: ☐ **Applied to next return** or ☐ **Refunded** ▶			9	

Part II Record of Quarterly Federal Unemployment Tax Liability (Do not include state liability.) **Complete only if line 6 is over $100.**

Quarter	First (Jan. 1 – Mar. 31)	Second (Apr. 1 – June 30)	Third (July 1 – Sept. 30)	Fourth (Oct. 1 – Dec. 31)	Total for year
Liability for quarter					

Third-Party Designee

Do you want to allow another person to discuss this return with the IRS (see the separate instructions)? ☐ **Yes.** Complete the following. ☐ **No**

Designee's name ▶ | Phone no. ▶ (   ) | Personal identification number (PIN) ▶

Under penalties of perjury, I declare that I have examined this return, including accompanying schedules and statements, and, to the best of my knowledge and belief, it is true, correct, and complete, and that no part of any payment made to a state unemployment fund claimed as a credit was, or is to be, deducted from the payments to employees.

Signature ▶ | **Title (Owner, etc.)** ▶ | **Date** ▶

For Privacy Act and Paperwork Reduction Act Notice, see the separate instructions. ▼ **DETACH HERE** ▼ Cat. No. 10983G Form **940-EZ**

Form **940-V(EZ)**

Department of the Treasury
Internal Revenue Service

Payment Voucher

Use this voucher only when making a payment with your return.

OMB No. 1545-1110

2019

Complete boxes 1, 2, and 3. Do not send cash, and do not staple your payment to this voucher. Make your check or money order payable to the "United States Treasury." Be sure to enter your employer identification number (EIN), "Form 940-EZ," and "2004" on your payment.

1 Enter your employer identification number (EIN).

2 **Enter the amount of your payment.** ▶ | Dollars | Cents

3 Enter your business name (individual name for sole proprietors).

Enter your address.

Enter your city, state, and ZIP code.

Copyright © 2017 by McGraw-Hill Education. All rights reserved.

Name ______________________

PROBLEM 11.6A or 11.6B

WORK CLASSIFICATION	ESTIMATED EARNINGS	INSURANCE RATE	ESTIMATED PREMIUMS

WORK CLASSIFICATION	ACTUAL EARNINGS	INSURANCE RATE	ACTUAL PREMIUMS

Copyright © 2017 by McGraw-Hill Education. All rights reserved.

Name

PROBLEM 11.6A or 11.6B (continued)

GENERAL JOURNAL PAGE

	DATE		DESCRIPTION	POST. REF.	DEBIT	CREDIT	
1							1
2							2
3							3
4							4
5							5
6							6
7							7
8							8
9							9
10							10
11							11
12							12
13							13
14							14
15							15
16							16
17							17
18							18
19							19

Analyze:

Copyright © 2017 by McGraw-Hill Education. All rights reserved.

Name

CRITICAL THINKING PROBLEM 11.1

1.

2.

3.

4.

5.

Analyze:

CRITICAL THINKING PROBLEM 11.2

1.

2. YEARLY COST—CURRENT SYSTEM

Copyright © 2017 by McGraw-Hill Education. All rights reserved.

Name

CRITICAL THINKING PROBLEM 11.2 (continued)

YEARLY COST—PROPOSED SYSTEM

3.

Copyright © 2017 by McGraw-Hill Education. All rights reserved.

WORKING PAPERS

Name ____________________

EXERCISE 12.1

GENERAL JOURNAL — PAGE______

	DATE		DESCRIPTION	POST. REF.	DEBIT	CREDIT	
1							1
2							2
3							3
4							4
5							5
6							6
7							7

EXERCISE 12.2

____

____

____

EXERCISE 12.3

GENERAL JOURNAL — PAGE______

	DATE		DESCRIPTION	POST. REF.	DEBIT	CREDIT	
1							1
2							2
3							3
4							4
5							5
6							6
7							7
8							8
9							9
10							10
11							11
12							12
13							13
14							14
15							15
16							16
17							17
18							18

Copyright © 2017 by McGraw-Hill Education. All rights reserved.

Name ____________________

EXERCISE 12.4

GENERAL JOURNAL PAGE________

	DATE		DESCRIPTION	POST. REF.	DEBIT	CREDIT	
1							1
2							2
3							3
4							4
5							5
6							6
7							7
8							8
9							9
10							10
11							11
12							12
13							13

EXERCISE 12.5

GENERAL JOURNAL PAGE________

	DATE		DESCRIPTION	POST. REF.	DEBIT	CREDIT	
1							1
2							2
3							3
4							4
5							5
6							6
7							7
8							8

EXERCISE 12.6

GENERAL JOURNAL PAGE________

	DATE		DESCRIPTION	POST. REF.	DEBIT	CREDIT	
1							1
2							2
3							3
4							4

Copyright © 2017 by McGraw-Hill Education. All rights reserved.

Name ______________________

EXERCISE 12.7

GENERAL JOURNAL PAGE______

	DATE		DESCRIPTION	POST. REF.	DEBIT	CREDIT	
1							1
2							2
3							3
4							4
5							5
6							6
7							7
8							8
9							9
10							10
11							11
12							12
13							13

Copyright © 2017 by McGraw-Hill Education. All rights reserved.

Name

PROBLEM 12.1A or 12.1B

GENERAL JOURNAL PAGE

	DATE	DESCRIPTION	POST. REF.	DEBIT	CREDIT	
1						1
2						2
3						3
4						4
5						5
6						6
7						7
8						8
9						9
10						10
11						11
12						12
13						13
14						14
15						15
16						16
17						17
18						18
19						19
20						20
21						21
22						22
23						23
24						24
25						25
26						26
27						27
28						28
29						29
30						30
31						31
32						32
33						33
34						34
35						35
36						36
37						37

Copyright © 2017 by McGraw-Hill Education. All rights reserved.

Name ____________________

PROBLEM 12.1A or 12.1B (continued)

GENERAL JOURNAL PAGE______

DATE	DESCRIPTION	POST. REF.	DEBIT	CREDIT

Analyze: ____________________

Copyright © 2017 by McGraw-Hill Education. All rights reserved.

Name

PROBLEM 12.2A or 12.2B

GENERAL JOURNAL PAGE 1

	DATE		DESCRIPTION	POST. REF.	DEBIT	CREDIT	
1							1
2							2
3							3
4							4
5							5
6							6
7							7
8							8
9							9
10							10
11							11
12							12
13							13
14							14
15							15
16							16
17							17
18							18
19							19
20							20
21							21
22							22
23							23
24							24
25							25
26							26
27							27
28							28
29							29
30							30
31							31
32							32
33							33
34							34
35							35
36							36
37							37

Copyright © 2017 by McGraw-Hill Education. All rights reserved.

Name ______________________

PROBLEM 12.2A or 12.2B (continued)

GENERAL JOURNAL PAGE 2

DATE		DESCRIPTION	POST. REF.	DEBIT	CREDIT

Analyze: ______________________

Copyright © 2017 by McGraw-Hill Education. All rights reserved.

Name ______________________

PROBLEM 12.3A or 12.3B

	ACCOUNT NAME	TRIAL BALANCE		ADJUSTMENTS	
		DEBIT	CREDIT	DEBIT	CREDIT
1					
2					
3					
4					
5					
6					
7					
8					
9					
10					
11					
12					
13					
14					
15					
16					
17					
18					
19					
20					
21					
22					
23					
24					
25					
26					
27					
28					
29					
30					
31					
32					

Copyright © 2017 by McGraw-Hill Education. All rights reserved.

Name ______________________

PROBLEM 12.3A or 12.3B (continued)

____

____

ADJUSTED TRIAL BALANCE		INCOME STATEMENT		BALANCE SHEET		
DEBIT	CREDIT	DEBIT	CREDIT	DEBIT	CREDIT	
						1
						2
						3
						4
						5
						6
						7
						8
						9
						10
						11
						12
						13
						14
						15
						16
						17
						18
						19
						20
						21
						22
						23
						24
						25
						26
						27
						28
						29
						30
						31
						32

Analyze: ______________________

Copyright © 2017 by McGraw-Hill Education. All rights reserved.

Name ______________________

PROBLEM 12.4A or 12.4B

	ACCOUNT NAME	TRIAL BALANCE		ADJUSTMENTS	
		DEBIT	CREDIT	DEBIT	CREDIT
1					
2					
3					
4					
5					
6					
7					
8					
9					
10					
11					
12					
13					
14					
15					
16					
17					
18					
19					
20					
21					
22					
23					
24					
25					
26					
27					
28					
29					
30					
31					
32					
33					
34					

Copyright © 2017 by McGraw-Hill Education. All rights reserved.

Name

PROBLEM 12.4A or 12.4B (continued)

ADJUSTED TRIAL BALANCE		INCOME STATEMENT		BALANCE SHEET	
DEBIT	CREDIT	DEBIT	CREDIT	DEBIT	CREDIT

Copyright © 2017 by McGraw-Hill Education. All rights reserved.

Name

PROBLEM 12.4A or 12.4B (continued)

	ACCOUNT NAME	TRIAL BALANCE		ADJUSTMENTS	
		DEBIT	CREDIT	DEBIT	CREDIT
1					
2					
3					
4					
5					
6					
7					
8					
9					
10					
11					
12					
13					
14					
15					
16					
17					
18					
19					
20					
21					
22					
23					
24					
25					
26					
27					
28					
29					
30					
31					
32					

Copyright © 2017 by McGraw-Hill Education. All rights reserved.

Name

PROBLEM 12.4A or 12.4B (continued)

Adjusted Trial Balance		Income Statement		Balance Sheet		
DEBIT	CREDIT	DEBIT	CREDIT	DEBIT	CREDIT	
						1
						2
						3
						4
						5
						6
						7
						8
						9
						10
						11
						12
						13
						14
						15
						16
						17
						18
						19
						20
						21
						22
						23
						24
						25
						26
						27
						28
						29
						30
						31
						32

Analyze:

Copyright © 2017 by McGraw-Hill Education. All rights reserved.

Name

PROBLEM 12.5A or 12.5B

	ACCOUNT NAME	TRIAL BALANCE DEBIT	TRIAL BALANCE CREDIT	ADJUSTMENTS DEBIT	ADJUSTMENTS CREDIT
1					
2					
3					
4					
5					
6					
7					
8					
9					
10					
11					
12					
13					
14					
15					
16					
17					
18					
19					
20					
21					
22					
23					
24					
25					
26					
27					
28					
29					
30					
31					
32					
33					
34					

Copyright © 2017 by McGraw-Hill Education. All rights reserved.

Name ______________________

PROBLEM 12.5A or 12.5B (continued)

	ADJUSTED TRIAL BALANCE		INCOME STATEMENT		BALANCE SHEET		
	DEBIT	CREDIT	DEBIT	CREDIT	DEBIT	CREDIT	
							1
							2
							3
							4
							5
							6
							7
							8
							9
							10
							11
							12
							13
							14
							15
							16
							17
							18
							19
							20
							21
							22
							23
							24
							25
							26
							27
							28
							29
							30
							31
							32
							33
							34

Copyright © 2017 by McGraw-Hill Education. All rights reserved.

Name

PROBLEM 12.5A or 12.5B (continued)

	ACCOUNT NAME	TRIAL BALANCE		ADJUSTMENTS	
		DEBIT	CREDIT	DEBIT	CREDIT
1					
2					
3					
4					
5					
6					
7					
8					
9					
10					
11					
12					
13					
14					
15					
16					
17					
18					
19					
20					
21					
22					
23					
24					
25					
26					
27					
28					
29					
30					
31					
32					

Copyright © 2017 by McGraw-Hill Education. All rights reserved.

Name ____________________

PROBLEM 12.5A or 12.5B (continued)

ADJUSTED TRIAL BALANCE		INCOME STATEMENT		BALANCE SHEET		
DEBIT	CREDIT	DEBIT	CREDIT	DEBIT	CREDIT	
						1
						2
						3
						4
						5
						6
						7
						8
						9
						10
						11
						12
						13
						14
						15
						16
						17
						18
						19
						20
						21
						22
						23
						24
						25
						26
						27
						28
						29
						30
						31
						32

Analyze: ____________________

Copyright © 2017 by McGraw-Hill Education. All rights reserved.

Name

PROBLEM 12.6A or 12.6B

	ACCOUNT NAME	TRIAL BALANCE		ADJUSTMENTS	
		DEBIT	CREDIT	DEBIT	CREDIT
1					
2					
3					
4					
5					
6					
7					
8					
9					
10					
11					
12					
13					
14					
15					
16					
17					
18					
19					
20					
21					
22					
23					
24					
25					
26					
27					
28					
29					
30					
31					
32					
33					
34					
35					

Copyright © 2017 by McGraw-Hill Education. All rights reserved.

Name ______________________________

PROBLEM 12.6A or 12.6B (continued)

	ADJUSTED TRIAL BALANCE		INCOME STATEMENT		BALANCE SHEET		
	DEBIT	CREDIT	DEBIT	CREDIT	DEBIT	CREDIT	
							1
							2
							3
							4
							5
							6
							7
							8
							9
							10
							11
							12
							13
							14
							15
							16
							17
							18
							19
							20
							21
							22
							23
							24
							25
							26
							27
							28
							29
							30
							31
							32
							33
							34
							35

Copyright © 2017 by McGraw-Hill Education. All rights reserved.

Name

CRITICAL THINKING PROBLEM 12.1

	ACCOUNT NAME	TRIAL BALANCE DEBIT	TRIAL BALANCE CREDIT	ADJUSTMENTS DEBIT	ADJUSTMENTS CREDIT
1					
2					
3					
4					
5					
6					
7					
8					
9					
10					
11					
12					
13					
14					
15					
16					
17					
18					
19					
20					
21					
22					
23					
24					
25					
26					
27					
28					
29					
30					
31					
32					
33					

Copyright © 2017 by McGraw-Hill Education. All rights reserved.

Name

CRITICAL THINKING PROBLEM 12.1 (continued)

	ADJUSTED TRIAL BALANCE		INCOME STATEMENT		BALANCE SHEET		
	DEBIT	CREDIT	DEBIT	CREDIT	DEBIT	CREDIT	
							1
							2
							3
							4
							5
							6
							7
							8
							9
							10
							11
							12
							13
							14
							15
							16
							17
							18
							19
							20
							21
							22
							23
							24
							25
							26
							27
							28
							29
							30
							31
							32
							33

Copyright © 2017 by McGraw-Hill Education. All rights reserved.

Name

CRITICAL THINKING PROBLEM 12.1 (continued)

	ACCOUNT NAME	TRIAL BALANCE DEBIT	TRIAL BALANCE CREDIT	ADJUSTMENTS DEBIT	ADJUSTMENTS CREDIT
1					
2					
3					
4					
5					
6					
7					
8					
9					
10					
11					
12					
13					
14					
15					
16					
17					
18					
19					
20					
21					
22					
23					
24					
25					
26					
27					
28					
29					
30					
31					
32					

Copyright © 2017 by McGraw-Hill Education. All rights reserved.

Name

CRITICAL THINKING PROBLEM 12.1 (continued)

ADJUSTED TRIAL BALANCE		INCOME STATEMENT		BALANCE SHEET		
DEBIT	CREDIT	DEBIT	CREDIT	DEBIT	CREDIT	
						1
						2
						3
						4
						5
						6
						7
						8
						9
						10
						11
						12
						13
						14
						15
						16
						17
						18
						19
						20
						21
						22
						23
						24
						25
						26
						27
						28
						29
						30
						31
						32

Copyright © 2017 by McGraw-Hill Education. All rights reserved.

Name

CRITICAL THINKING PROBLEM 12.1 (continued)

GENERAL JOURNAL

PAGE 30

DATE		DESCRIPTION	POST. REF.	DEBIT	CREDIT

Copyright © 2017 by McGraw-Hill Education. All rights reserved.

Name ______________________

CRITICAL THINKING PROBLEM 12.1 (continued)

GENERAL JOURNAL PAGE 32

DATE	DESCRIPTION	POST. REF.	DEBIT	CREDIT

Copyright © 2017 by McGraw-Hill Education. All rights reserved.

Name

CRITICAL THINKING PROBLEM 12.1 (continued)

a. Net Sales

b. Net Delivered Cost of Purchases

c. Cost of Goods Sold

d. Net Income (from worksheet)

e. Capital, December 31

Analyze:

Copyright © 2017 by McGraw-Hill Education. All rights reserved.

Name

CRITICAL THINKING PROBLEM 12.2

1.

2.

Copyright © 2017 by McGraw-Hill Education. All rights reserved.

WORKING PAPERS

Name ______________________________

EXERCISE 13.1

1. Purchases Returns and Allowances ____________
2. Telephone Expense ____________
3. Sales Returns and Allowances ____________
4. Purchases ____________
5. Interest Income ____________
6. Merchandise Inventory ____________
7. Interest Expense ____________
8. Sales ____________
9. Depreciation Expense—Store Equipment ____________
10. Rent Expense ____________
11. Sales Discounts ____________
12. Supplies Expense ____________
13. Freight In ____________
14. Purchases Discounts ____________
15. Uncollectible Accounts Expense ____________

EXERCISE 13.2

1. Accounts Receivable ____________
2. Delivery Van ____________
3. Prepaid Insurance ____________
4. Notes Payable, due 2025 ____________
5. Store Supplies ____________
6. Accounts Payable ____________
7. Merchandise Inventory ____________
8. David Stafford, Capital ____________
9. Cash ____________
10. Unearned Subscription Income ____________
11. Notes Receivable, due 2020 ____________
12. Accumulated Depreciation—Van ____________
13. Notes Payable, 2020 ____________
14. David Stafford, Drawing ____________
15. Interest Payable

EXERCISE 13.3

(continued)

Copyright © 2017 by McGraw-Hill Education. All rights reserved.

Name

EXERCISE 13.3 (continued)

EXERCISE 13.4

Copyright © 2017 by McGraw-Hill Education. All rights reserved.

Name

EXERCISE 13.5

Copyright © 2017 by McGraw-Hill Education. All rights reserved.

Name ____________________

EXERCISE 13.6

GENERAL JOURNAL PAGE________

DATE	DESCRIPTION	POST. REF.	DEBIT	CREDIT

Copyright © 2017 by McGraw-Hill Education. All rights reserved.

Name ____________________

EXERCISE 13.7

GENERAL JOURNAL PAGE ______

DATE		DESCRIPTION	POST. REF.	DEBIT	CREDIT

Copyright © 2017 by McGraw-Hill Education. All rights reserved.

Name ______________________________

EXERCISE 13.8

ACCOUNT NAME	DEBIT	CREDIT

Copyright © 2017 by McGraw-Hill Education. All rights reserved.

Name

EXERCISE 13.9

a. Net Sales is

Gross profit is

The gross profit percentage is

b. Current assets are

Current liabilities are

Working capital is

Copyright © 2017 by McGraw-Hill Education. All rights reserved.

Name ______________________

EXERCISE 13.9 (continued)

c. The current ratio is ______________________

d. The inventory turnover is ______________________

e. The accounts receivable turnover is ______________________

EXERCISE 13.10

a.

b.

Copyright © 2017 by McGraw-Hill Education. All rights reserved.

Name

PROBLEM 13.1A or 13.1B

(continued)

Copyright © 2017 by McGraw-Hill Education. All rights reserved.

Name

PROBLEM 13.1A or 13.1B (continued)

Copyright © 2017 by McGraw-Hill Education. All rights reserved.

Name

PROBLEM 13.1A or 13.1B (continued)

(continued)

Copyright © 2017 by McGraw-Hill Education. All rights reserved.

Name

PROBLEM 13.1A or 13.1B (continued)

Analyze:

Copyright © 2017 by McGraw-Hill Education. All rights reserved.

Name

PROBLEM 13.2A or 13.2B

(continued)

Copyright © 2017 by McGraw-Hill Education. All rights reserved.

Name

PROBLEM 13.2A or 13.2B (continued)

Copyright © 2017 by McGraw-Hill Education. All rights reserved.

Name

PROBLEM 13.2A or 13.2B (continued)

(continued)

Copyright © 2017 by McGraw-Hill Education. All rights reserved.

Name

PROBLEM 13.2A or 13.2B (continued)

Analyze:

Copyright © 2017 by McGraw-Hill Education. All rights reserved.

Name

PROBLEM 13.3A or 13.3B

(continued)

Copyright © 2017 by McGraw-Hill Education. All rights reserved.

Name

PROBLEM 13.3A or 13.3B (continued)

Copyright © 2017 by McGraw-Hill Education. All rights reserved.

Name

PROBLEM 13.3A or 13.3B (continued)

(continued)

Copyright © 2017 by McGraw-Hill Education. All rights reserved.

Name

PROBLEM 13.3A or 13.3B (continued)

Analyze:

Copyright © 2017 by McGraw-Hill Education. All rights reserved.

Name

PROBLEM 13.4A or 13.4B

GENERAL JOURNAL PAGE

	DATE		DESCRIPTION	POST. REF.	DEBIT	CREDIT	
1							1
2							2
3							3
4							4
5							5
6							6
7							7
8							8
9							9
10							10
11							11
12							12
13							13
14							14
15							15
16							16
17							17
18							18
19							19
20							20
21							21
22							22
23							23
24							24
25							25
26							26
27							27
28							28
29							29
30							30
31							31
32							32
33							33
34							34
35							35
36							36
37							37

Copyright © 2017 by McGraw-Hill Education. All rights reserved.

Name ____________________

PROBLEM 13.4A or 13.4B (continued)

GENERAL JOURNAL PAGE ________

	DATE	DESCRIPTION	POST. REF.	DEBIT	CREDIT	
1						1
2						2
3						3
4						4
5						5
6						6
7						7
8						8
9						9
10						10
11						11
12						12
13						13
14						14
15						15
16						16
17						17
18						18
19						19
20						20
21						21
22						22
23						23
24						24
25						25
26						26
27						27
28						28
29						29
30						30
31						31
32						32
33						33
34						34
35						35
36						36
37						37

Copyright © 2017 by McGraw-Hill Education. All rights reserved.

Name

PROBLEM 13.4A or 13.4B (continued)

GENERAL JOURNAL

PAGE

DATE		DESCRIPTION	POST. REF.	DEBIT	CREDIT

Copyright © 2017 by McGraw-Hill Education. All rights reserved.

Name

PROBLEM 13.4A or 13.4B (continued)

GENERAL JOURNAL

PAGE

DATE	DESCRIPTION	POST. REF.	DEBIT	CREDIT

Analyze:

PAGE

DATE	DESCRIPTION	POST. REF.	DEBIT	CREDIT

Copyright © 2017 by McGraw-Hill Education. All rights reserved.

Name ____________________

PROBLEM 13.5A or 13.5B

GENERAL JOURNAL PAGE ______

DATE	DESCRIPTION	POST. REF.	DEBIT	CREDIT

Copyright © 2017 by McGraw-Hill Education. All rights reserved.

Name ______________________

PROBLEM 13.5A or 13.5B (continued)

GENERAL JOURNAL PAGE______

	DATE	DESCRIPTION	POST. REF.	DEBIT	CREDIT	
1						1
2						2
3						3
4						4
5						5
6						6
7						7
8						8
9						9
10						10
11						11
12						12
13						13
14						14
15						15
16						16

Analyze: ______________________

EXTRA FORM

GENERAL JOURNAL PAGE______

	DATE	DESCRIPTION	POST. REF.	DEBIT	CREDIT	
1						1
2						2
3						3
4						4
5						5
6						6
7						7
8						8
9						9
10						10
11						11
12						12
13						13

Copyright © 2017 by McGraw-Hill Education. All rights reserved.

Name

CRITICAL THINKING PROBLEM 13.1

	ACCOUNT NAME	TRIAL BALANCE		ADJUSTMENTS	
		DEBIT	CREDIT	DEBIT	CREDIT
1					
2					
3					
4					
5					
6					
7					
8					
9					
10					
11					
12					
13					
14					
15					
16					
17					
18					
19					
20					
21					
22					
23					
24					
25					
26					
27					
28					
29					
30					
31					
32					
33					
34					
35					
36					

Copyright © 2017 by McGraw-Hill Education. All rights reserved.

Name ______________________

CRITICAL THINKING PROBLEM 13.1 (continued)

____

____

	ADJUSTED TRIAL BALANCE		INCOME STATEMENT		BALANCE SHEET		
	DEBIT	CREDIT	DEBIT	CREDIT	DEBIT	CREDIT	
							1
							2
							3
							4
							5
							6
							7
							8
							9
							10
							11
							12
							13
							14
							15
							16
							17
							18
							19
							20
							21
							22
							23
							24
							25
							26
							27
							28
							29
							30
							31
							32
							33
							34
							35
							36

Copyright © 2017 by McGraw-Hill Education. All rights reserved.

Name ______________________

CRITICAL THINKING PROBLEM 13.1 (continued)

Copyright © 2017 by McGraw-Hill Education. All rights reserved.

Name

CRITICAL THINKING PROBLEM 13.1 (continued)

EXTRA FORM

Copyright © 2017 by McGraw-Hill Education. All rights reserved.

Name

CRITICAL THINKING PROBLEM 13.1 (continued)

Copyright © 2017 by McGraw-Hill Education. All rights reserved.

Name ______________________

CRITICAL THINKING PROBLEM 13.1 (continued)

GENERAL JOURNAL PAGE________

DATE	DESCRIPTION	POST. REF.	DEBIT	CREDIT

Copyright © 2017 by McGraw-Hill Education. All rights reserved.

Name ______________________________

CRITICAL THINKING PROBLEM 13.1 (continued)

GENERAL JOURNAL

PAGE ________

DATE	DESCRIPTION	POST. REF.	DEBIT	CREDIT

Copyright © 2017 by McGraw-Hill Education. All rights reserved.

Name ______________________

CRITICAL THINKING PROBLEM 13.1 (continued)

GENERAL JOURNAL PAGE______

	DATE		DESCRIPTION	POST. REF.	DEBIT	CREDIT	
1							1
2							2
3							3
4							4
5							5
6							6
7							7
8							8
9							9
10							10
11							11
12							12
13							13
14							14
15							15
16							16
17							17
18							18
19							19
20							20
21							21
22							22
23							23
24							24
25							25
26							26
27							27
28							28
29							29
30							30
31							31
32							32
33							33
34							34
35							35
36							36
37							37

Copyright © 2017 by McGraw-Hill Education. All rights reserved.

Name ______________________________

CRITICAL THINKING PROBLEM 13.1 (continued)

GENERAL JOURNAL — PAGE ______

DATE		DESCRIPTION	POST. REF.	DEBIT	CREDIT

Analyze: ______________________________

Copyright © 2017 by McGraw-Hill Education. All rights reserved.

Name

CRITICAL THINKING PROBLEM 13.2

1.

2.

Copyright © 2017 by McGraw-Hill Education. All rights reserved.

Name

CHAPTER 13 CRITICAL THINKING PROBLEM (continued)

3.

Copyright © 2017 by McGraw-Hill Education. All rights reserved.

MINI-PRACTICE SET 2

Name

Merchandising Business Accounting Cycle

SALES JOURNAL

PAGE

	DATE		SALES SLIP NO.	CUSTOMER'S NAME	POST. REF.	ACCOUNTS RECEIVABLE DEBIT	SALES TAX PAYABLE CREDIT	SALES CREDIT	
1									1
2									2
3									3
4									4
5									5
6									6
7									7
8									8
9									9
10									10
11									11
12									12
13									13
14									14

PURCHASES JOURNAL

PAGE

DATE		PURCHASED FROM	INVOICE NUMBER	INVOICE DATE	TERMS	POST. REF.	PURCHASES DR./ ACCOUNTS PAYABLE CREDIT

Copyright © 2017 by McGraw-Hill Education. All rights reserved.

 Name ____________________

CASH RECEIPTS JOURNAL

PAGE____

DATE	DESCRIPTION	POST. REF.	ACCOUNTS RECEIVABLE CREDIT	SALES TAX PAYABLE CREDIT	SALES CREDIT	OTHER ACCOUNTS CREDIT			CASH DEBIT
						ACCOUNT NAME	POST. REF.	AMOUNT	

Copyright © 2017 by McGraw-Hill Education. All rights reserved.

 Name ____________________

CASH PAYMENTS JOURNAL

PAGE____

DATE	CK. NO.	DESCRIPTION	POST. REF.	ACCOUNTS PAYABLE DEBIT	OTHER ACCOUNTS DEBIT			PURCHASES DISCOUNTS CREDIT	CASH CREDIT
					ACCOUNT NAME	POST. REF.	AMOUNT		

Copyright © 2017 by McGraw-Hill Education. All rights reserved.

 Name

GENERAL JOURNAL PAGE

	DATE	DESCRIPTION	POST. REF.	DEBIT	CREDIT	
1						1
2						2
3						3
4						4
5						5
6						6
7						7
8						8
9						9
10						10
11						11
12						12
13						13
14						14
15						15
16						16
17						17
18						18
19						19
20						20
21						21
22						22
23						23
24						24
25						25
26						26
27						27
28						28
29						29
30						30
31						31
32						32
33						33
34						34
35						35
36						36
37						37
38						38

Copyright © 2017 by McGraw-Hill Education. All rights reserved.

MINI-PRACTICE SET 2 (continued)

Name ____________________

GENERAL JOURNAL

PAGE ________

DATE	DESCRIPTION	POST. REF.	DEBIT	CREDIT

Copyright © 2017 by McGraw-Hill Education. All rights reserved.

Name ______________________

GENERAL JOURNAL

PAGE ______

DATE		DESCRIPTION	POST. REF.	DEBIT	CREDIT

Copyright © 2017 by McGraw-Hill Education. All rights reserved.

Name ____________________

GENERAL LEDGER

ACCOUNT ____________________ ACCOUNT NO. ________

DATE		DESCRIPTION	POST. REF.	DEBIT	CREDIT	BALANCE	
						DEBIT	CREDIT

ACCOUNT ____________________ ACCOUNT NO. ________

DATE		DESCRIPTION	POST. REF.	DEBIT	CREDIT	BALANCE	
						DEBIT	CREDIT

ACCOUNT ____________________ ACCOUNT NO. ________

DATE		DESCRIPTION	POST. REF.	DEBIT	CREDIT	BALANCE	
						DEBIT	CREDIT

ACCOUNT ____________________ ACCOUNT NO. ________

DATE		DESCRIPTION	POST. REF.	DEBIT	CREDIT	BALANCE	
						DEBIT	CREDIT

Copyright © 2017 by McGraw-Hill Education. All rights reserved.

 Name ____________________

GENERAL LEDGER

ACCOUNT ____________________ ACCOUNT NO. ________

DATE		DESCRIPTION	POST. REF.	DEBIT	CREDIT	BALANCE DEBIT	BALANCE CREDIT

ACCOUNT ____________________ ACCOUNT NO. ________

DATE		DESCRIPTION	POST. REF.	DEBIT	CREDIT	BALANCE DEBIT	BALANCE CREDIT

ACCOUNT ____________________ ACCOUNT NO. ________

DATE		DESCRIPTION	POST. REF.	DEBIT	CREDIT	BALANCE DEBIT	BALANCE CREDIT

ACCOUNT ____________________ ACCOUNT NO. ________

DATE		DESCRIPTION	POST. REF.	DEBIT	CREDIT	BALANCE DEBIT	BALANCE CREDIT

ACCOUNT ____________________ ACCOUNT NO. ________

DATE		DESCRIPTION	POST. REF.	DEBIT	CREDIT	BALANCE DEBIT	BALANCE CREDIT

Copyright © 2017 by McGraw-Hill Education. All rights reserved.

 Name ______________________

GENERAL LEDGER

ACCOUNT ______________________ ACCOUNT NO. ________

DATE		DESCRIPTION	POST. REF.	DEBIT	CREDIT	BALANCE DEBIT	BALANCE CREDIT

ACCOUNT ______________________ ACCOUNT NO. ________

DATE		DESCRIPTION	POST. REF.	DEBIT	CREDIT	BALANCE DEBIT	BALANCE CREDIT

ACCOUNT ______________________ ACCOUNT NO. ________

DATE		DESCRIPTION	POST. REF.	DEBIT	CREDIT	BALANCE DEBIT	BALANCE CREDIT

ACCOUNT ______________________ ACCOUNT NO. ________

DATE		DESCRIPTION	POST. REF.	DEBIT	CREDIT	BALANCE DEBIT	BALANCE CREDIT

Copyright © 2017 by McGraw-Hill Education. All rights reserved.

 Name ______________________

GENERAL LEDGER

ACCOUNT ______________________ ACCOUNT NO. ________

DATE		DESCRIPTION	POST. REF.	DEBIT	CREDIT	BALANCE	
						DEBIT	CREDIT

ACCOUNT ______________________ ACCOUNT NO. ________

DATE		DESCRIPTION	POST. REF.	DEBIT	CREDIT	BALANCE	
						DEBIT	CREDIT

ACCOUNT ______________________ ACCOUNT NO. ________

DATE		DESCRIPTION	POST. REF.	DEBIT	CREDIT	BALANCE	
						DEBIT	CREDIT

ACCOUNT ______________________ ACCOUNT NO. ________

DATE		DESCRIPTION	POST. REF.	DEBIT	CREDIT	BALANCE	
						DEBIT	CREDIT

ACCOUNT ______________________ ACCOUNT NO. ________

DATE		DESCRIPTION	POST. REF.	DEBIT	CREDIT	BALANCE	
						DEBIT	CREDIT

Copyright © 2017 by McGraw-Hill Education. All rights reserved.

 Name ____________________

GENERAL LEDGER

ACCOUNT ____________________ ACCOUNT NO. ________

DATE		DESCRIPTION	POST. REF.	DEBIT	CREDIT	BALANCE DEBIT	BALANCE CREDIT

ACCOUNT ____________________ ACCOUNT NO. ________

DATE		DESCRIPTION	POST. REF.	DEBIT	CREDIT	BALANCE DEBIT	BALANCE CREDIT

ACCOUNT ____________________ ACCOUNT NO. ________

DATE		DESCRIPTION	POST. REF.	DEBIT	CREDIT	BALANCE DEBIT	BALANCE CREDIT

ACCOUNT ____________________ ACCOUNT NO. ________

DATE		DESCRIPTION	POST. REF.	DEBIT	CREDIT	BALANCE DEBIT	BALANCE CREDIT

Copyright © 2017 by McGraw-Hill Education. All rights reserved.

 Name

GENERAL LEDGER

ACCOUNT ______ ACCOUNT NO. ______

DATE		DESCRIPTION	POST. REF.	DEBIT	CREDIT	BALANCE	
						DEBIT	CREDIT

ACCOUNT ______ ACCOUNT NO. ______

DATE		DESCRIPTION	POST. REF.	DEBIT	CREDIT	BALANCE	
						DEBIT	CREDIT

ACCOUNT ______ ACCOUNT NO. ______

DATE		DESCRIPTION	POST. REF.	DEBIT	CREDIT	BALANCE	
						DEBIT	CREDIT

ACCOUNT ______ ACCOUNT NO. ______

DATE		DESCRIPTION	POST. REF.	DEBIT	CREDIT	BALANCE	
						DEBIT	CREDIT

ACCOUNT ______ ACCOUNT NO. ______

DATE		DESCRIPTION	POST. REF.	DEBIT	CREDIT	BALANCE	
						DEBIT	CREDIT

Copyright © 2017 by McGraw-Hill Education. All rights reserved.

 Name ______________________

GENERAL LEDGER

ACCOUNT ______________________ ACCOUNT NO. ________

DATE		DESCRIPTION	POST. REF.	DEBIT	CREDIT	BALANCE	
						DEBIT	CREDIT

ACCOUNT ______________________ ACCOUNT NO. ________

DATE		DESCRIPTION	POST. REF.	DEBIT	CREDIT	BALANCE	
						DEBIT	CREDIT

ACCOUNT ______________________ ACCOUNT NO. ________

DATE		DESCRIPTION	POST. REF.	DEBIT	CREDIT	BALANCE	
						DEBIT	CREDIT

ACCOUNT ______________________ ACCOUNT NO. ________

DATE		DESCRIPTION	POST. REF.	DEBIT	CREDIT	BALANCE	
						DEBIT	CREDIT

ACCOUNT ______________________ ACCOUNT NO. ________

DATE		DESCRIPTION	POST. REF.	DEBIT	CREDIT	BALANCE	
						DEBIT	CREDIT

Copyright © 2017 by McGraw-Hill Education. All rights reserved.

 Name ____________

GENERAL LEDGER

ACCOUNT ____________ ACCOUNT NO. ________

DATE	DESCRIPTION	POST. REF.	DEBIT	CREDIT	BALANCE DEBIT	BALANCE CREDIT

ACCOUNT ____________ ACCOUNT NO. ________

DATE	DESCRIPTION	POST. REF.	DEBIT	CREDIT	BALANCE DEBIT	BALANCE CREDIT

ACCOUNT ____________ ACCOUNT NO. ________

DATE	DESCRIPTION	POST. REF.	DEBIT	CREDIT	BALANCE DEBIT	BALANCE CREDIT

ACCOUNT ____________ ACCOUNT NO. ________

DATE	DESCRIPTION	POST. REF.	DEBIT	CREDIT	BALANCE DEBIT	BALANCE CREDIT

ACCOUNT ____________ ACCOUNT NO. ________

DATE	DESCRIPTION	POST. REF.	DEBIT	CREDIT	BALANCE DEBIT	BALANCE CREDIT

Copyright © 2017 by McGraw-Hill Education. All rights reserved.

 Name ____________________

ACCOUNTS RECEIVABLE SUBSIDIARY LEDGER

NAME ____________________ TERMS ________

DATE		DESCRIPTION	POST. REF.	DEBIT	CREDIT	BALANCE

NAME ____________________ TERMS ________

DATE		DESCRIPTION	POST. REF.	DEBIT	CREDIT	BALANCE

NAME ____________________ TERMS ________

DATE		DESCRIPTION	POST. REF.	DEBIT	CREDIT	BALANCE

NAME ____________________ TERMS ________

DATE		DESCRIPTION	POST. REF.	DEBIT	CREDIT	BALANCE

NAME ____________________ TERMS ________

DATE		DESCRIPTION	POST. REF.	DEBIT	CREDIT	BALANCE

Copyright © 2017 by McGraw-Hill Education. All rights reserved.

 Name ______________________________

ACCOUNTS RECEIVABLE SUBSIDIARY LEDGER

NAME ______________________________ TERMS __________

DATE		DESCRIPTION	POST. REF.	DEBIT	CREDIT	BALANCE

NAME ______________________________ TERMS __________

DATE		DESCRIPTION	POST. REF.	DEBIT	CREDIT	BALANCE

ACCOUNTS PAYABLE SUBSIDIARY LEDGER

NAME ______________________________ TERMS __________

DATE		DESCRIPTION	POST. REF.	DEBIT	CREDIT	BALANCE

NAME ______________________________ TERMS __________

DATE		DESCRIPTION	POST. REF.	DEBIT	CREDIT	BALANCE

Copyright © 2017 by McGraw-Hill Education. All rights reserved.

MINI-PRACTICE SET 2 (continued)

Name ______________________

ACCOUNTS PAYABLE SUBSIDIARY LEDGER

NAME ______________________ TERMS ____________

DATE		DESCRIPTION	POST. REF.	DEBIT	CREDIT	BALANCE

Copyright © 2017 by McGraw-Hill Education. All rights reserved.

MINI-PRACTICE SET 2 (continued)

Name

	ACCOUNT NAME	TRIAL BALANCE DEBIT	TRIAL BALANCE CREDIT	ADJUSTMENTS DEBIT	ADJUSTMENTS CREDIT
1					
2					
3					
4					
5					
6					
7					
8					
9					
10					
11					
12					
13					
14					
15					
16					
17					
18					
19					
20					
21					
22					
23					
24					
25					
26					
27					
28					
29					
30					
31					
32					
33					
34					
35					
36					

Copyright © 2017 by McGraw-Hill Education. All rights reserved.

MINI-PRACTICE SET 2 (continued)

Name ______________________________

ADJUSTED TRIAL BALANCE		INCOME STATEMENT		BALANCE SHEET		
DEBIT	CREDIT	DEBIT	CREDIT	DEBIT	CREDIT	
						1
						2
						3
						4
						5
						6
						7
						8
						9
						10
						11
						12
						13
						14
						15
						16
						17
						18
						19
						20
						21
						22
						23
						24
						25
						26
						27
						28
						29
						30
						31
						32
						33
						34
						35
						36

Copyright © 2017 by McGraw-Hill Education. All rights reserved.

Name ______________________

	ACCOUNT NAME	TRIAL BALANCE		ADJUSTMENTS	
		DEBIT	CREDIT	DEBIT	CREDIT
1					
2					
3					
4					
5					
6					
7					
8					
9					
10					
11					
12					
13					
14					
15					
16					
17					
18					
19					
20					
21					
22					
23					
24					
25					
26					
27					
28					
29					
30					
31					
32					
33					
34					
35					
36					

Copyright © 2017 by McGraw-Hill Education. All rights reserved.

MINI-PRACTICE SET 2 (continued)

Name ____________________

ADJUSTED TRIAL BALANCE		INCOME STATEMENT		BALANCE SHEET	
DEBIT	CREDIT	DEBIT	CREDIT	DEBIT	CREDIT

Copyright © 2017 by McGraw-Hill Education. All rights reserved.

Name

Copyright © 2017 by McGraw-Hill Education. All rights reserved.

 Name

Copyright © 2017 by McGraw-Hill Education. All rights reserved.

MINI-PRACTICE SET 2 (continued)

Name

Copyright © 2017 by McGraw-Hill Education. All rights reserved.

 Name

ACCOUNT NAME	DEBIT	CREDIT

Copyright © 2017 by McGraw-Hill Education. All rights reserved.

MINI-PRACTICE SET 2 (continued)

Name ____________________

EXTRA FORMS

	ACCOUNT NAME	TRIAL BALANCE		ADJUSTMENTS	
		DEBIT	CREDIT	DEBIT	CREDIT
1					
2					
3					
4					
5					
6					
7					
8					
9					
10					
11					
12					
13					
14					
15					
16					
17					
18					
19					
20					
21					
22					
23					
24					
25					
26					
27					
28					
29					
30					
31					
32					
33					
34					

Copyright © 2017 by McGraw-Hill Education. All rights reserved.

 Name ______________________

ADJUSTED TRIAL BALANCE		INCOME STATEMENT		BALANCE SHEET	
DEBIT	CREDIT	DEBIT	CREDIT	DEBIT	CREDIT

Copyright © 2017 by McGraw-Hill Education. All rights reserved.

MINI-PRACTICE SET 2 (continued)

Name ______________________

EXTRA FORM

GENERAL JOURNAL

PAGE ________

DATE	DESCRIPTION	POST. REF.	DEBIT	CREDIT

Copyright © 2017 by McGraw-Hill Education. All rights reserved.